A Mother's Love For Her
Miracle Twins
A true story of prematurity, hope, love and 133 days

Narelle Wyrsch

First published by Busybird Publishing 2018
Copyright © 2018 Narelle Wyrsch

ISBN
Print: 978-1-925830-07-1
Ebook: 978-1-925830-08-8

Narelle Wyrsch has asserted her right under the Copyright, Designs and Patents Act 1988 to be identified as the author of this work. The information in this book is based on the author's experiences and opinions. The publisher specifically disclaims responsibility for any adverse consequences, which may result from use of the information contained herein. Permission to use information has been sought by the author. Any breaches will be rectified in further editions of the book.

All rights reserved. No part of this publication may be reproduced, stored in or introduced into a retrieval system, or transmitted in any form, or by any means (electronic, mechanical, photocopying, recording or otherwise) without the prior written permission of the author. Any person who does any unauthorised act in relation to this publication may be liable to criminal prosecution and civil claims for damages. Enquiries should be made through the publisher.

Cover design: Busybird Publishing
Layout and typesetting: Busybird Publishing
Editor: Samantha Allemann

Busybird Publishing
2/118 Para Road
Montmorency, Victoria
Australia 3094
www.busybird.com.au

*This book is dedicated to my amazing daughters,
Hailey and Amy,
who continue to inspire me day after day.*

Contents

Prologue	i
Introduction	1
1. Birth day and first month in hospital	7
2. Month 2 – June 1998	27
3. Month 3 – July 1998	59
4. Month 4 – August 1998	79
5. Month 5 – September 1998	95
6. Milestones	101
7. Conclusion	103
8. Where are they now?	111

Prologue

Unable to fall pregnant naturally, I found myself at the age of twenty-seven about to embark on IVF treatment. With IVF still being relatively new and not knowing anyone who had been through it, I didn't know what to expect. After an unsuccessful initial attempt at IVF, we were very lucky to fall pregnant on our second attempt. Both times we opted to have three fertilised embryos transferred directly into my uterus. I was also naive to the fact that babies could be born prematurely, especially not just over halfway through a pregnancy. Not only did we have to face the emotions of IVF, but then prematurity saw us call Monash Medical Centre our home for almost five months.

This is a diary journal of my joy at being pregnant, the birth of my daughters and the days and months that followed in hospital.

Introduction

Monday 8 December 1997

The pregnancy blood test was done first thing in the morning at Monash IVF but we had to wait until 3.30 pm for the results. Brad slept most of the day and I spent the day with Mum.

I was in a very glum mood as I was afraid of another negative result. Deep down I had a feeling I was pregnant, but I kept it to myself.

Brad made the call to our nurse at the clinic as I wasn't up to it. All I could hear him say was 'is she ... really?' and I had to grab the phone. It was confirmed I was finally pregnant. When we hung up the phone we hugged each other and cried.

We rang our families and a few special friends to share the news. We had a lot of celebrating and planning to do.

Monday 22 December 1997

We're at the six-week stage and it's time for the ultrasound, to see how many embryos from the three implanted have taken.

The sonographer found our first baby's heart and confirmed it was beating at 100 beats per minute. Then she found our second baby's heart, also beating at 100 beats per minute. Brad and I looked at each other with tears in our eyes – we are having twins!

We feel so lucky to be the proud parents-to-be of twins.

Saturday 31 January 1998 (12 weeks pregnant)

After a very anxious wait, we have finally hit the twelve-week stage. I have been feeling very tired and had bouts of nausea on and off, but I don't want to complain. My belly's growing and I'm very proud of it.

Brad and I haven't stopped smiling since the pregnancy was confirmed; we hope we will have a happy family.

Our next ultrasound is on Tuesday and I'm very excited about that. We're looking forward to seeing how the babies are developing.

Tuesday 3 February 1998

Wow, what a buzz! The ultrasound appointment was at 8 am and took an hour. The sonographer had a look at our babies, then proceeded to take all the vital measurements. Twin One was good; a bit active but okay. Twin Two would not stop moving about.

It was amazing watching the TV monitor and seeing our babies moving so much and not being able to feel it on the outside (that I can't wait for).

It was a very special moment for Brad and I, to find out that both babies were healthy with all the vital organs and arms and legs. One of the babies put their hand up close enough so we could count their fingers.

There were tears of happiness and I felt so proud of what Brad and I had achieved in creating these two beautiful babies – our children.

Friday 13 February 1998

I walked past a baby shop at Forest Hill Chase Shopping Centre that was having a sale and decided to have a look. I saw some lovely Teddy Bear Picnic T-shirts for six month old babies. I decided to buy one for each of the babies.

So, my beautiful babies, this is my first gift to you, apart from my eternal love. I felt so proud bringing the T-shirts home and putting them away for when you fit into them.

Saturday 14 March 1998 (18 weeks pregnant)

Time appears to be progressing very quickly. I saw my obstetrician during the week and he is very pleased with both babies' progress.

We've slowly started to get things organised at home. The bedroom for the babies has been cleaned out and we're looking at getting new doors on the robe. We put two cots on lay-by the other week and I'm looking forward to getting them home so we can set-up the room.

I have been feeling butterfly movements in my tummy for a little while now, and look forward to feeling some kicking soon.

The eighteen-week ultrasound is on Tuesday and we will get a video of it. It will be great to see how the babies have developed since the last scan.

Tuesday 17 March 1998

Wow! What an exciting morning. We went to Monash Private Hospital at 9 am for our ultrasound. It was so exciting; both babies were moving about a lot.

The ultrasound took about an hour and a half. We had a good look at both babies and the sonographer took all their vital measurements and checked feet and hands. All was well and she told us we are expecting two perfectly healthy and beautiful babies.

Brad and I watched the TV monitor and I couldn't believe it was my tummy and babies we were watching. It was all very exciting and hard to put into words, the feelings and love we had watching you both.

We got a video of the ultrasound and I watched it in the evening with Mum. She was so happy and excited to be able to see the babies, and can't wait to hold them when they are born.

I hope one day our babies realise how special they are to us. We know they will make us very happy. They are our dream that we thought might never come true, but always wanted.

Thursday 23 April 1998 (23 weeks pregnant)

I've been feeling both babies kicking and moving about for a while now. Twin Two is a lot more active than Twin One. I often wonder if this is a sign of things to come.

Brad's been fantastic in his support, and quite eager to feel the babies for himself. Well, today was the day. I was lying down and Brad put his hand on my tummy. He was quite emotional when he felt Twin Two kicking through my tummy. He got a faint movement from Twin One.

Brad was thrilled by it all, and I was happy because he finally got the chance to share with me this special feeling.

Tuesday 28 April 1998 (24 weeks 3 days pregnant)

What an emotionally draining day today was. When I awoke in the morning, things appeared to be fine, so I got myself organised and went to work. What I didn't know was that I may not be home for quite some time.

At work I was experiencing quite a heavy discharge, so I rang the hospital and explained it to them, then rang Dr Lawrence's surgery. Dr Lawrence's secretary rang the hospital and they decided I should go there to be checked out.

At Waverley Private Hospital, they put me on the fetal monitor to check the babies' heartbeats and they were going strong. My discharge was checked and I was told that I had ruptured my membrane (basically my water had broken).

I was admitted to Waverley, then transferred by ambulance to Jessie McPherson Private Hospital at the Monash Medical Centre. By this stage I was emotionally worn out. My concern was for the health and wellbeing of the babies.

Brad met me at Jessie McPherson, and was naturally beside himself with worry about me and our precious babies. Not much can be done now except complete bed rest in the hope the membrane may repair itself.

I've been told that I will not go home until the babies are born. Well, I hope to be here for a long time, to keep nurturing the babies in my tummy. I'll dearly miss Brad and our home, but I know the longer I'm in hospital, the better it is for our precious children.

Birth day and first month in hospital

Tuesday 5 May 1998 (25 weeks 3 days pregnant)

I knew this morning there was something special about today. Last night I had a high temperature and cold shivers, and this morning I had a high temperature and hot sweats. I couldn't eat much and was experiencing a discharge.

Dr Lawrence came in and examined me about 1.30 pm, and advised I had developed an infection and 'we need to deliver the babies today to avoid risking any danger to them'.

I broke into tears and rang Brad to tell him the news. He was at the hospital in about twenty minutes. I certainly didn't want to risk our babies, and knew delivering today was giving them a chance, even though it is so early. I have faith in the medical team at Monash and know they will do what they can for the babies.

I was taken to the labour ward (delivery room) about 3.30 pm and monitored. I had a steroid injection (to assist with the babies' lungs) and had an IV put in my arm to feed fluid through. An epidural was put into my back (that hurt) and a catheter tube into my bladder, connected to a bag (for wee).

Mum and Brad were with me, and I could see the pain in their eyes as I cried tears of pain and fear. I felt contractions about five minutes apart. Dr Lawrence checked my progress and found my cervix wasn't opening quick enough and one of the babies was ready to be born.

We had to decide if we wanted to proceed and possibly risk the first baby, or have a caesarean, which would put me at risk because of having surgery with an unknown infection, but the babies would be okay. Brad and I opted for an emergency caesarean.

I was taken off the IV drip (which had a drug coming through it to induce labour) and taken directly to theatre. Brad got into hospital gear while I was dosed up with more local anaesthetic through the epidural. Mum waited outside, and Brad and I went into theatre feeling very anxious and nervous. Dr Lawrence, the midwives, paediatricians and nurses acted very quickly. I was awake but didn't feel anything.

They cut my lower abdomen and took out the first baby. We heard a little whimper and were told 'it's a girl'. We named her Hailey Narelle. The neonatal team took her straight away and started monitoring her.

The second baby came out a minute later and also let out a whimper. Another girl, Amy Lorraine. She was also checked and monitored straight away. Brad watched it all and was speechless because our babies, although tiny, were so perfect.

I was given a quick glance of Amy before being taken to recovery, where I cried as I realised Brad and I have two beautiful daughters to love and cherish. Mum and Brad came into recovery and were both overcome with the miracle of it all. I was taken back to my room in a very drugged daze and was given a polaroid photo of each of the girls, which I look at all the time.

Brad and I feel so lucky and proud to have two such special daughters. We'll love and cherish our girls for eternity.

	Hailey Narelle	**Amy Lorraine**
Time:	9.33 pm	9.34 pm
Weight:	670 grams	592 grams
Length:	30 cm	30 cm
Head circumference:	22 cm	22 cm

Wednesday 6 May 1998

Brad stayed with me last night which was great. When I awoke I was still in a daze about how quickly everything happened yesterday. One thing I could focus on was that Brad and I were parents to two beautiful daughters.

I was confined to bed as I was still hooked up to the epidural, IV and catheter bag. I was wheeled on my bed to the neonatal intensive care unit (NICU) where the girls were. They may be tiny but they are perfect and beautiful; a true show of Brad and my love for each other.

We are unable to hold or touch the girls at this stage, but we will as soon as we can. Both girls are in plastic bags on warm mats and ventilated with oxygen support. It is quite overwhelming to see, as they are so tiny, with all these big machines around them.

I spent the rest of the day in my room. We had a few visitors, which helped pass the day and slightly ease the pain I was feeling of not being close to Hailey and Amy. Brad saw the girls when he could and showed them off to family and friends who visited. Brad stayed the night because I was feeling helpless towards the girls, should they need me.

Thursday 7 May 1998

I am finally off all the drips that have kept me confined to bed. I am feeling a lot of pain from the caesarean, but not as much pain as not being able to hold or touch my babies. The only way I can get around is in a wheelchair. I managed about four trips to see the girls today.

Amy has developed jaundice, so she is under phototherapy lights, with netting over her eyes. The nurses think her eyes are still fused shut, but the netting will protect them if not. So far everything else is going well for Amy. She had a small blood transfusion which is to be expected, being so delicate.

Hailey is also progressing well. I think she already has her daddy wrapped around her finger. She responds to Brad's voice and often opens her eyes when she hears its. This is a good sign, because usually at this stage the eyes are still fused shut.

Hailey is breathing quite a bit on her own. The evening nurse said she is such a sweet thing. Brad and I were able to touch her and she responded positively when I touched her skin. It is so soft and she actually grasped my finger. Hailey had a small blood transfusion also today.

No one can give any guarantees on the progress of Amy or Hailey. We just have to take each day as it comes. The love Brad and I have for our little girls is unexplainable; an emotion I thought never possible.

Friday 8 May 1998

I'm still feeling very weak, and got the morning off to a bad start with tears of frustration at not being able to do anything for the girls. The paediatricians are happy with both girls' progress which is encouraging to hear.

Hailey has now developed jaundice too, so she is also under the phototherapy lights. She has netting covering her beautiful eyes.

Her blood pressure is still a bit low and they are keeping a close eye on this. The nurses reported she is in a stable condition.

Amy has still got the jaundice so the lights are still on her. Everything else with Amy is stable.

Brad is starting to get very frustrated with the situation, because he wants to protect his family and feels everything at the moment is out of his control.

Saturday 9 May 1998

Brad has been wonderful. He has spent every day at the hospital with us. We are still trying to spend as much time as possible with the girls, but the wound from my caesarean is very sore and I get uncomfortable quickly. We've had visitors every day which has been nice and they've brought some lovely flowers, gifts and cards for us and the girls.

Amy is still stable except for the jaundice. Her movements have slowed down a bit, which is good, because she was wriggling so much and knocking her monitors off. I still haven't been able to touch Amy yet, because we haven't been there at the right time when she's having her care done.

Hailey has had the phototherapy light for her jaundice turned off. She has still been experiencing low blood pressure, and one of the paediatricians explained to us what has occurred. When a baby is in your tummy, it has a natural hole (flap) in the heart where nutrients, blood, etc., are passed through. At birth, this hole fuses shut and the baby's heart operates as it should. Often in premature babies, this fusing does not occur and subsequently this results in low blood pressure or other setbacks.

They are putting a drug through Hailey to try and fix this problem. A small amount of Morphine is also being administered to Hailey to try and slow down her wriggling and interference with the monitors.

In the evening, Hailey's blood pressure appeared to have stabilised.

Sunday 10 May 1998 (Mother's Day)

My very first Mother's Day. What a wonderful joy to celebrate today as the mother of two beautiful girls. Brad came into the hospital early, and with his mum, plotted a nice surprise for me.

I got organised and Brad wheeled me to NICU to see our girls. The doctors were in Amy's room, so we went to see Hailey. She was unwrapped, and I burst into tears and went and washed my hands so I could touch my little girl. She was so soft and quite relaxed. There was a flower and card for me from Hailey, which I know Brad had a hand in organising. The ward staff also had a card for me from Hailey.

We finally got to see Amy, and there was also a beautiful flower and card from her. How lucky I am to have such a thoughtful husband and daughters. The ward staff had also left a card for me from Amy.

As I still hadn't touched Amy, I decided today was my day. I washed my hands and the nurses lifted the plastic so I could put my hand through and touch her gently. What beautiful soft skin. I cried as I finally got to touch my second baby for the first time.

The days seem to be rolling into one. There were a few visitors today and we spent a few hours chatting with Hailey and Amy. I know I talked a lot when they were in my tummy, so I want them to continue to hear my voice as often as possible.

Hailey has developed jaundice again, so is under the phototherapy light. Her blood pressure is also a bit low, so a slow dose of the necessary drug is being administered into her.

She is being weaned off the Morphine because it was affecting her breathing. The machine to assist Hailey's breathing gives her so many breaths and then she needs to breathe the rest on her own. The Morphine wasn't allowing her brain to do this. The nurse with her today is very pleased with her and said that she appears to be the most stable since she was born.

Amy is still under the light for jaundice. Her breathing and blood pressure appear to be going along quite steadily. She is also stable and resting nicely. Both girls are on the same machines, but their progress is monitored individually.

Generally, when a baby is born their weight is made up also of water. Over the first couple of days, the weight drops. Following the weight drop, premature babies should gain about 20-30 grams per day. Babies who are premature like Hailey and Amy stay in 'plastic bags' on warm mats to try and create the illusion of being in the womb. These bags humidify the air.

After a period of time, the bag is taken off but the babies stay on the warm mats. Once the babies get to around 1000 grams, they are put into Isolettes (incubators), which still have assisted breathing, etc., but babies can be touched easier. They wear nappies and clothes. The final step is an open cot.

In NICU, where the babies are, there are seven bays. Bays 6 and 7 are intensive care (Amy is in 6 and Hailey is in 7), and as the babies get stronger, they progress to the next bay. Bays 1 and 2 are fattening-up areas. It is expected the girls will be in 6 and 7 for about eight weeks.

The average time to get the babies home is their due date, 14 August. If no complications arise, they should be home by then, or if they do well, maybe a little earlier.

The girls will probably have to fight a few infections, and by the time they come home will have had quite a few doses of antibiotics.

Monday 11 May 1998

I can't believe the girls are six days old today. I still think back to two weeks ago when I left for work and landed in hospital. What an anxious, frightening and very happy two weeks they have been.

I had my staples out this morning, so hopefully I will be able to get around a bit more. I'm still in a bit of pain from the operation, but that should ease soon. Brad and I went and saw the girls in the morning and received some positive news from one of the senior paediatricians.

Amy is still coming along well. Her blood pressure has been stable. Hopefully she might start on some milk today. 1 ml every four hours; hopefully she will digest it. Her blood levels will be checked for jaundice and, if all okay, she might have the light turned off today. She hasn't experienced the low blood pressure like Hailey, although it still could happen.

Hailey has had her light for jaundice turned off again. She is still on the drug for the blood pressure, but has responded so well that the dose has been dropped from 1.2 ml to 0.5 ml through the IV. Her blood will be tested again in the afternoon to check her levels.

The paediatrician is pleased at how 'remarkably well' both girls have come along. We cross our fingers that they continue to thrive as they have.

In the evening, Amy started taking my milk (which I have been expressing since the girls were born), just a small amount, and is digesting it well, which is fantastic. I finally feel like I'm doing something for the girls.

Hailey's blood pressure is still stable and all other levels are okay. The nurse has put a nappy on her to try and stop her wriggling so much. It also looks very cute.

Tuesday 12 May 1998 (1 week old)

Brad went and saw the girls first thing in the morning on his way home from work – his first night back since Hailey and Amy were born.

Amy had an unsettled night. Her blood pressure dropped but appears to have stabilised. Amy has had the jaundice light turned off. I was in her room at the right time, and got to wipe her bottom after a wee and changed the nappy under her. I know it's not much, but for me it was a very special thing. Hailey has been doing a few bowel movements and is now also trying 1 ml every four hours of my milk. She is still wriggling about all the time.

Both girls have had the humidity bag removed from over them. They now have a flat plastic sheet over the bed to keep the warmth in.

The nurses are telling me so much about the girls' progress that I have so many things going around in my head. I'm trying to remember everything I can, but I know I will forget a few things.

In the evening, Mum and I were admiring Hailey in a nappy when I saw her do her first vomit. I panicked seeing this, but the nurses said it is quite common. Babies aren't meant to use their own functions at twenty-six-weeks' gestation, as they depend on the mum to do the work for them. However, premature babies are encouraged to start using their own functions as soon as possible, to adapt them to the outside world.

Amy still hasn't opened her bowels and her tummy is getting quite full.

Wednesday 13 May 1998

I'm still feeling pain from the caesarean, but I think I might be going home tomorrow which I'm dreading as I will have to leave my babies in hospital, however I know they're in good hands. I won't be able to drive for a couple of weeks so I will have to depend on others to bring me to the hospital.

I bought the girls their first present from me since they were born. One pink and one white knitted cardigan for them to share. They will probably fit when they are about six to eight months old. I think I'm going to like buying things for my two girls.

Amy's tummy is still a bit distended and she hasn't opened her bowels yet. She was given an enema last night, so hopefully this may make things happen. Hailey has stopped having milk at this stage. She is using her bowels but is also vomiting a bit. I think her hair has grown and is also turning lighter.

Amy now has one of her eyes open. I was touching her and putting my finger in her hand and she was pushing her fingers into mine. She kept looking at me and I was feeling such love for her.

Hailey has still been vomiting but they are trying her on a bit of milk again. She is opening her eyes a lot too and it makes me melt.

Thursday 14 May 1998

Today I am going home from hospital. I have mixed emotions. I don't want to leave my babies, but I want to be home with Brad, preparing for the girls' homecoming. Hopefully the girls will be home in three months.

Hailey had a good night and is now digesting my milk well. She hasn't had any more vomits and they are thinking of increasing her milk intake. The nurse said she is in an excellent condition.

Amy is still experiencing a few problems with the same heart condition as Hailey had. At this stage they won't give her any drugs in the hope it will fix itself. She still hasn't opened her bowels. Amy also has a nappy on now. Her right eye is now also open.

I feel such pride when I look at the girls. They are little battlers and very strong. It breaks our hearts seeing all the tubes in them, but it is vital for them to be able to survive.

I came home from hospital about 4 pm, feeling very empty without my girls. I spent the rest of the afternoon sorting through my things and putting all of our 'congratulations' flowers in vases.

We got a call from the nursery about 6.30 pm and my heart sank, thinking something was wrong with Hailey or Amy. They were ringing to advise Hailey was moved from Bay 7 to Bay 6 so now she is with Amy. I'm much happier having both girls in the same room.

Amy is having problems with her oxygen levels and has had a blood test to establish what is wrong. She might have an infection or perhaps the flap in her heart is causing problems. Either way, she will have a course of drugs.

Hailey has settled into her new temporary home well. She is having a bit more milk but hasn't been keeping it down. It's a case of trying these things to encourage their bodies to work for themselves. She was weighed today and has put on nine grams, now weighing 679 grams.

Both girls are opening their eyes when they hear our voices, which makes my heart melt all the time.

Friday 15 May 1998

My first night at home was an anxious one as I worried about the girls.

Hailey is continuing to do well. I got to change her nappy for the first time today, which was great. Her ventilation has been cut down and if she responds well she could be moved into an Isolette when one becomes available. This means we can start to massage her. She was sleeping on her tummy today and looked very comfortable.

Amy had a very unstable night. Her oxygen level went up to about 60% when it should be below 40%. She was a bit more stable during the day. She has started on the medication to correct her heart. There have been a few other tests done to check different things. Amy is being monitored closely by the doctors and nurses, which is reassuring when she goes up and down all the time.

I changed Hailey's nappy today and helped change Amy's. I know the road ahead is a long one, but getting the girls home is my number one priority.

Saturday 16 May 1998

Hailey is continuing to do well. Her ventilator has been turned back up a bit, but this is not a problem. She did a poo this morning and managed to somehow get it on her ankle. She doesn't like sitting in a wet nappy; she lifts her legs and bottom to try and avoid it.

Amy is still up and down with her oxygen. She has been taken off milk for a couple of days as she is on a course of drugs.

The nurses are saying both girls have healthy looking skin and look healthy within themselves. This is encouraging to hear.

Sunday 17 May 1998

Amy is still the same with her oxygen level. She was taken off the drug for the heart flap because it was affecting her weeing (a side effect of the drug). During the day she did some wee, so I think they are going to give her the next course of the drug during the night.

I'm getting concerned for Amy, as she appears to have a battle ahead of her. Hailey is still doing well. She is now on 1 ml every two hours of milk.

I've been changing both girls' nappies if I've been at the hospital at the right time. This has meant a lot to me.

Monday 18 May 1998

I can't believe it's been thirteen days since the girls were born. I hope the next thirteen weeks go as quickly. I'm spending about four hours during the day and two hours at night at the hospital with the girls. I like to be with them; watching, talking and reading books to them.

Both girls are stable and no changes from yesterday. They did have a brain scan today (they check for blood clots or losses and any abnormalities) and both were perfect.

Tuesday 19 May 1998 (2 weeks old)

Two weeks have passed since the girls were born. It's been a mixed period of emotions; absolute joy to have two beautiful daughters, and heartache at the struggle they have ahead of them.

Hailey is stable and continuing to do well. The nurse asked me if I would like to hold her today and I struggled to hold back my tears of joy. They got Hailey out of the open cot and put her in my arms and wrapped her warmly. She held my finger and we sat there together for nearly two hours.

Hailey was very relaxed and the nurse was pleased with how she responded to being held by me. I certainly enjoyed it. Whilst I was holding her, the nurses changed her bed over from an open cot with a plastic sheet to an enclosed Isolette. This is a good sign that Hailey is doing well.

Amy is unfortunately a bit unstable at the moment. She is still up and down with her oxygen requirements. She is being started on 1 ml every four hours of milk again. She is on her third (I think) dose of the drug to repair the flap in the heart.

Amy had some physio today to open her lungs more. This appears to have helped. She doesn't like having her care done and plays up a bit, however she responds well to her physio and my touch.

Wednesday 20 May 1998

What a joy it was to come into the hospital this morning and see that Amy had also been transferred to an Isolette. She appears to be more stable. The physio has helped her, and the drug for the heart flap has helped stabilise her also.

Amy opened her bowels for the first time overnight, twice, and both times there was quite a bit of poo. Her oxygen has been lower, which is good. She is now up to 1 ml of milk every two hours.

Hailey is stable and often in 100% air (not requiring any oxygen support), which is good. She had a comfortable night and appears to be happy in her Isolette. She was weighed today and now weighs 710 grams. At midnight Hailey's feeds are being increased to 1 ml every hour.

Thursday 21 May 1998

Today was another special day for me. I had my first hold of Amy. She was very relaxed and appeared to be happy with our hour together. She was weighed today and now weighs 639 grams – a weight gain of forty-seven grams since birth (Hailey's gain was forty grams since birth).

She is stabilising, which is good, and occasionally went into 100% air during the day. Her ventilator has been dropped a bit. The ventilator breathes the set number of breaths per minute and the babies have to do the rest themselves. The goal is to get the girls off the ventilator and oxygen as soon as possible.

Hailey is still stable and often in 100% air. Her ventilator has been turned down also.

Amy will be changing to 1 ml every hour of milk at midnight.

Friday 22 May 1998

Hailey is looking very relaxed when she is sleeping. Her milk intake has been increased to 2 ml every hour and will possibly be increased to 3 ml every hour tonight.

Amy is still stable, and when I came in this morning she was in 100% air, which was great. She was laying on her tummy with her head facing to the left and was a bit unsettled, so she had her head moved to face right and was much happier. Her blood test showed signs of infection, so she is on some antibiotics.

Saturday 23 May 1998

Amy is doing well and is often in 100% air. Her ventilator is at 15. She is continuing to have physio and this appears to be helping her. She will be on her course of antibiotics for about a week. Amy's milk intake has been increased to 2 ml every hour. She is also on steroids to help develop her lungs.

Hailey is resting well and is in 100% air most of the time. Her ventilator has been turned down to a minimum rate of 10. I had another lovely cuddle with her today. It was only for about half an hour but it was a very special half hour. She was very good whilst I was holding her.

Hailey was weighed again today and her weight is 695 grams (a drop from last week). The difference in weight could be attributed to time of day of weighing, if she had just done a wee, or a few other factors. It's not a concern at this stage. She will be weighed again in a couple of days.

Sunday 24 May 1998

Hailey's milk intake has been increased to 4 ml every hour and she is tolerating this nicely. She has had quite a few secretions in her nose and throat, and a sample of these has been sent off to be checked for any signs of infection. Her ventilator was increased to 15 overnight. I changed her nappy today and she had yellow poos. This is progression.

Amy has had a settled but rough day. She had a lumbar puncture done to check fluid in her spine for signs for meningitis. I waited for the results and they were fine. Thank goodness. Her protein level was a bit high so they will keep an eye on this. Her milk intake was stopped overnight but is being recommenced at 6 pm, back on 2 ml every hour.

Monday 25 May 1998
Hailey 689 grams / Amy 624 grams

Amy has had her antibiotics cut down which is good. I had another special cuddle with her today and gave her a sponge bath, using cotton balls and a face washer for a towel. She appeared quite relaxed for the rest of the day.

Hailey has had her milk increased to 5 ml every hour and is having an additive with it to help her gain weight. She hasn't been tolerating the additive very well, but they are persisting with it. Hailey is having a blood transfusion today as she is a bit anaemic.

I've been changing both girls' nappies as often as I can.

Tuesday 26 May 1998 (3 weeks old)

I had another nice surprise when I arrived today. Hailey has had her IV taken out as she is not on any antibiotics or medication at the moment. Her hair is certainly thickening up and is a light brown colour.

Amy is still on 2 ml every hour of milk. This hasn't been increased because she didn't appear to be digesting it, however, this morning she has had a couple of bowel movements, so hopefully they increase her milk intake. She currently has IVs in both arms. Amy's hair is more of a honey blonde.

Both girls have had their ventilators dropped to 10, so hopefully they will respond positively.

Amy's feeds are going up to 3 ml every hour tonight. If she tolerates this, she will have one of her IVs and drips removed within the next couple of days.

I had a hold of Hailey in the afternoon which was lovely.

Wednesday 27 May 1998

Hailey 693 grams

I enjoy spending time with the girls and watching their personalities develop. Hailey likes to stretch out when she sleeps, whereas Amy scrunches herself up. Hailey appears happiest sleeping on her tummy, and for Amy, it's her left side. Hailey doesn't mind being touched, and Amy gets very grisly when touched. Amy does enjoy her physio though, and when she recognises my touch she is quite relaxed.

I'm having my first real social outing today, lunch with a friend, which I'm feeling a bit apprehensive about. I know I'll miss the girls like crazy, but I'm sure they won't notice too much that I'm missing.

Amy's feeds are going up to 4 ml every hour sometime later today/tonight. She has had one of her IVs removed because her arm has tissued and is quite swollen. At this stage, they won't be replacing the IV. She is now on two courses of antibiotics, one to fight the infection in her blood and the other is a preventative because she has a few bruises.

Hailey has had a good day. She is tolerating her feeds well.

The nurse with the girls tonight was commenting on how strong they are and that they should now continue to grow and work their way up through the Bays.

Thursday 28 May 1998

Amy 615 grams

Hailey has had her ventilator dropped to 5. If she responds well, the doctors will pull one of her tubes out of her lungs this afternoon. This means we will be able to hear her cry. It's all trial and error, and if she doesn't respond the first time, the tube will go back in and they will try again in the next couple of days.

Amy still has a little way to go to catch up to Hailey. She had a chest X-ray done today to check her lungs and a blood test to check her infections. She is tolerating her feeds well at the moment. Once she gets over the infections and finishes on the antibiotics she should start to put weight on quicker.

The love I have for Hailey and Amy is a feeling I never knew possible. It is a complete and unconditional love that only a mother can understand. They are my world.

Amy's chest X-ray shows her lungs are still a bit hazy, so she needs the assistance of the ventilator for a little longer. She is having a blood transfusion today to replace blood that has been taken for testing.

Hailey has now had the tubes pulled out of her lungs. I got to see her face for the first time without tape on it and it is very pretty. How nice it is to see her without any IVs or tubes in her.

A short tube has been put in to push air through to open her lungs, however she is breathing on her own. We will now be able to hear her cry. Hailey really is doing very well. We now have to encourage Amy along.

One of the doctors today was saying how well the girls are doing, which is extremely encouraging to hear.

Friday 29 May 1998

What a nice surprise I got when I came into the hospital this morning. Amy has now also had the long tube removed and short tube put in. I am so disappointed that I didn't get to see her pretty face without all the tape.

The nurses said she was very pleased to have the long tube out. Hopefully she will respond well, if not they will need to put the long tube back in to ventilate her for a little longer. So far she has responded well. Hailey is continuing to respond well to the short tube.

As much as I don't want the girls to cry, I'm looking forward to hearing them cry, which is made possible by having the short tube instead of the long tube.

I had a lovely hold of Amy today, and when she first came out of her Isolette she let out some beautiful sounds, tears. She soon settled in my arms and fell asleep again.

In the evening I had a lovely hold of Hailey. Hailey looks like she is filling out.

Both the girls need plenty of sleep and food to help them grow quicker. If both girls continue to be stable, I should be able to have a hold of each of them every day or every second day. It's beneficial for them to be held, almost as much as I love holding them.

Saturday 30 May 1998

Hailey 750 grams / Amy 642 grams

Both girls were weighed today and have put on quite a bit of weight, which is excellent.

Hailey is having a blood transfusion today as she is still showing signs of anaemia. Amy is still on two lots of antibiotics but hopefully they might finish soon.

I was able to have a hold of both girls today. It's great that they are both now stable enough for me to hold. If they look like they are in a deep sleep, I try not to disturb them, which is hard because I want to hold them all the time.

Sunday 31 May 1998

Hailey and Amy are both still on the short tube, which means they are breathing on their own. Their oxygen requirements have been fluctuating between air and about 30%. This appears to be okay, because they are working harder for themselves (no more machines to assist them with their breathing). Hopefully within a couple of weeks they may not need any oxygen at all, and the nose tubes can be removed all together.

I had a cuddle with Hailey today which was lovely.

There is a chance both girls may have reflux, because they are not digesting all their food. The nurses and doctors will keep an eye on them.

Amy is now also having fortifier added to her milk to help her put on weight quicker.

Month 2

June 1998

Monday 1 June 1998
Hailey 762 grams

Both girls have been saturating quite low overnight, which means at times they are forgetting to breathe. They have had the short tube changed from 2.5mm thick to 3mm thick to allow a greater air flow.

Hailey was particularly unstable overnight with her breathing, so she had a blood test done in the morning to check for infection. The test results showed she has an infection, so she has been put on antibiotics. She has had her feeds ceased at this stage and is being fed by an IV drip. Hopefully the antibiotics will assist her, if not, she might have to have the long tube put back in to stabilise her breathing.

In the evening, Hailey was given a tube in her mouth to expel the air from her tummy. She has also been given some ventilation to assist her with breathing. I hope she stabilises overnight now she has been started on antibiotics.

I had a lovely evening cuddle with Amy, which made me very happy.

Tuesday 2 June 1998 (4 weeks old)
Amy 684 grams

It was a delight to come into the hospital this morning to see Amy without any IVs in her arms or legs. She was sleeping peacefully, so I'm sure she's happier feeling freedom. She is still desaturating a bit, which means there is a prolonged pause in her breathing. This can cause the heart to slow, in response to low blood oxygen levels, so Amy is still requiring a bit of oxygen.

Hailey had a much better night. Her saturation and breathing improved dramatically. The ventilation has been turned off and she has been in air most of the day. The antibiotics have definitely helped her. Her milk feeds will start again when she is more stable.

Amy had her tube taken out to be changed, and it was found that her nose has been quite traumatised by the tube. I saw her beautiful face for the first time without tape, and it was everything and more than I expected. She had the tube put back in her other nostril and the feeding tube has been put through her mouth. This change in tube appears to be helping her saturation. She is still having her physio twice a day.

In the afternoon, Hailey had a lumbar puncture done to check for meningitis infection. The test results were fine.

Amy had a chest X-ray to check her lungs. They are still a bit hazy, which is possibly why she is requiring so much oxygen.

Wednesday 3 June 1998
Hailey 720 grams

Amy has still been requiring oxygen and desaturating a bit. They are doing all they can to avoid putting the long tube back in. She is having some extra medicine to assist the lungs and continuing with physio twice a day. She is also having a top-up of blood today as she has had a bit taken lately for blood tests. Amy has had a cannula put back in her arm; hopefully it will be out when the blood has gone through.

Hailey is still doing well with her breathing and saturation, and is in air most of the time. The antibiotics have definitely helped her. She is starting back on milk today, 1 ml every two hours. Her weight has dropped about forty grams since Monday. Hopefully when the milk feeds increase she will put weight on again rapidly.

Amy had another chest X-ray in the afternoon and it showed that her lungs are looking better. She has still been desaturating a lot and requiring oxygen. She has been given some ventilation to help her breathe. I'm sure by the morning she'll be back on the long tube.

I had a most wonderful experience this afternoon. I did 'kangaroo care' with Hailey. I cried as I felt her skin against mine for the first time. It was a very special moment for both of us.

In the evening, Amy was still experiencing problems with breathing and oxygen requirements. She has had a long tube put back in. Apparently this is not a setback, but being so small, she has just got tired and is finding it difficult to breathe for herself at this stage. They tell me that this happens with a lot of babies. She has had her feeds ceased at this stage until she is more stable.

I feel so guilty that both girls are struggling like this; I should still be protecting them in my tummy.

Thursday 4 June 1998

Amy has been much better with her breathing since she had the long tube put back in. She has been in air a lot of the time. She still has an IV in her arm and is being fed via a drip.

Hailey is still doing well with her breathing and the short tube, not requiring oxygen. The doctors are talking about taking the tube out altogether in a couple of days for her to breathe on her own.

Amy is being recommenced on milk at 2 ml every hour. Hailey is now on 1 ml every hour.

Friday 5 June 1998 (1 month old)
Hailey 761 grams / Amy 694 grams

What another nice surprise I got when I came into the hospital this morning. Hailey has had her nasal prong taken out and is breathing on her own. It will probably go back in, but they will see how long she can cope on her own. Her milk intake is still 1 ml every hour.

Amy has still been catching up with her breathing. She is ventilated at 25 and requiring up to about 30% oxygen. Her feeds have been increased to 3ml hourly and fortified.

I had a lovely hold of Hailey today. It was great to hold her without any tubes in her nose. She was very good and slept beautifully in my arms.

Both girls have put on around 100 grams since birth.

Saturday 6 June 1998 (30-weeks gestation)

Amy is still having a few problems with her breathing and desaturation. Her ventilator has been turned up to 30. The nurses are going to try not to handle her too much today, to give her a chance to sleep. Her milk feeds have been increased to 4 ml hourly. She is on antibiotics to fight off any infections and is having blood tests done to check her levels for different things.

Hailey is still breathing on her own. When I came into the hospital this morning I expected her to back on the nasal prong requiring a bit of oxygen, but she wasn't. She has done really well to be breathing on her own for so long, considering she is still quite small. Her face is so beautiful without all the tape on it; I can't stop looking at it. Her feeds are still at 1 ml hourly because they don't want her to have to work too hard too soon with digestion and breathing.

I was desperate for a hold of Amy today, but because she is a bit unstable we thought it best not to unsettle her. Hopefully tomorrow I can cuddle her. I did manage another cuddle with Hailey today which was nice.

Both girls have developed their own personalities and are a lot of fun to watch. Hailey is still a wriggler and uses her strength to wave her arms and legs about. Amy is more placid and scrunches herself up when she sleeps.

Sunday 7 June 1998

Hailey 821 grams

Hailey is still breathing on her own, but has been requiring a little bit of oxygen. They are talking about putting the nasal prong back in to help her for a little while. Considering how premature and small she was, she has done remarkably well breathing on her own. The bigger she grows, the stronger her lungs are becoming. Her feeds have been increased to 2 ml hourly.

Amy had another chest X-ray today to check her lungs. They are still a bit hazy. The doctors don't want to give her more steroids to assist in lung development because they have side effects. Her oxygen requirements have been quite high. Amy is on antibiotics and they are waiting for the results of the blood tests to see if there is a bug growing, causing an infection. It could be one of a lot of things that are making her unwell.

The doctors are keeping a close eye on Amy to determine exactly what is wrong. She has been a bit more active today and stretching out, whereas yesterday she was constantly scrunching herself up. She certainly looks like she's putting on weight and grown in length.

Brad had his first special hold of both Hailey and Amy tonight, which he thought was just wonderful. I also had a hold of Amy to which she responded well (so did I).

Monday 8 June 1998
Amy 760 grams

Amy is slowly improving. They are running tests to check if she has reflux, as her chest X-ray is showing her lungs are still a bit hazy. As a last resort she will be given a course of steroids to help with lung development.

Hailey's antibiotics have been stopped today. She is having a top-up of blood and her feeds have been increased to 3 ml hourly.

I had a hold of Amy in the afternoon which was lovely. She also had a blood top-up in the afternoon. I wanted to hold Hailey tonight, but she was sleeping peacefully and I didn't want to disturb her.

Tuesday 9 June 1998 (5 weeks old)
Hailey 858 grams

Hailey is still doing well with her breathing. It has been five days since she had the nasal prong removed and has been breathing on her own. I gave her a sponge bath today and we put some clothes on her – a tiny cream and green jumpsuit. She looks very cute and seems quite happy to be dressed.

Amy is still the same. They are doing more tests on her to check for infections and reflux. She is more active than she was a couple of days ago and now won't stop wriggling. Hailey may also need testing for reflux.

I had a nice hold of Hailey in the afternoon. At midnight her feeds are being increased to 4 ml hourly.

Wednesday 10 June 1998

I had a phone call at home in the morning to tell us that Hailey had been moved to Bay 5, and is now out of intensive care and into special care. Hopefully she will continue to work her way up the Bays. If she gets an infection she may need to move back Bays, but let's hope not.

Hailey has been requiring a small amount of oxygen in her cot but no breathing assistance. I did kangaroo care with Hailey in the afternoon, which was lovely and I think beneficial for both of us.

I'm still feeling concerned for Amy, as her oxygen requirements have been going quite high. They did another chest X-ray today and I'm pretty sure she will have another course of steroids. They have stopped her antibiotics, as her blood tests were not showing any signs of infection. She looks so peaceful and beautiful when she sleeps.

Amy's chest X-ray shows that her lungs are looking hazier. The blood tests haven't shown any infections. Her main pressure has been turned up to allow more air to push through to open up her lungs and assist her breathing.

They are going to do a heart echo tomorrow to check if the heart flap has re-opened, and if so they will give her the required drugs. If this has not happened, they will start her on steroids to help develop the lungs.

The quicker Amy puts on weight, the stronger her lungs will become. They want to wean her off the ventilator as soon as possible. At the moment, it looks like a slow road for Amy, but hopefully she will pick up quickly once the lung problem has been solved.

Thursday 11 June 1998

Hailey 870 grams / Amy 824 grams

Amy's feeds have been increased to 5 ml hourly. She had a bad night with high oxygen requirements. They will do another chest X-ray this morning to see what's happening. I hope they establish the exact problem with Amy's lungs soon so she can be started on the necessary drugs.

Hailey appears happy in Bay 5. She is now dressed in a fluoro yellow suit which fits her quite well. Her feeds have been increased to 5 ml hourly also. She has had the IV from her arm removed, so she is once again free from IVs in all arms and legs. She has been requiring a small amount of oxygen in her cot, but her breathing has been okay.

Amy's chest X-ray was a bit better than yesterday. They will do a heart echo in the next couple of days to check her heart. She is having a top-up of blood, as her level was a bit low. Her temperature has been a bit high so I hope she doesn't have another infection.

I'm so proud of how both girls are doing.

Friday 12 June 1998

Hailey has been requiring about 23-25% cot oxygen so they have increased her dosage of Theophylline. This is a caffeine-based drug and will help her with breathing and saturation.

Amy is still the same with her oxygen requirements and breathing. Her ventilator has been turned up to 45. She has been put on steroids to help with lung maturity. She will stay on the steroids until her lungs are okay. I'm pleased that finally something is happening to help her. We should notice an improvement by tomorrow afternoon.

Amy has been moved into a new Isolette, as the one she was in had a door fall off it. I hope she is happy in her new bed. They did some more tests on her to check for infection and they all came back with negative results, which is good.

Both girls have beautiful natures, and every time I look at them I just want to bundle them in my arms and smother them with kisses and cuddles.

Amy had her heart echo done in the evening and it showed that the heart duct (flap) is definitely closed. At least that's okay, we just have to work on the lungs. She has also had all her IVs removed so she can now move about a bit more freely.

Saturday 13 June 1998
Hailey 882 grams / Amy 835 grams

Amy's been getting up to a bit of mischief this morning. She pulled her feeding tube out of her tummy. The steroids appear to be helping her. Her ventilator has been turned down to 30 and her oxygen requirements have been dropping. She has had Theophylline stopped at the moment as her breathing has been good.

Hailey has been doing well and has been in air for quite a bit of the day. Her feeds have been increased to 6 ml hourly, and she has started on a drug to help her absorb the milk better because she was doing a few small vomits overnight. Her weight gain has been a bit slow, so if she keeps her feeds down today they will start fortifying her milk.

Amy has been started on vitamins which will also help her.

Sunday 14 June 1998

Hailey's oxygen requirements have been creeping up. I hope she's not getting tired of breathing; if so she may need assistance from one of the machines for a little while. If she stopped moving about all the time, she would have more energy to breathe. Her feeding tube has been placed in her mouth, leaving her nostrils free for breathing, in an attempt to help her.

Amy is still showing small signs of improvement since she started on the steroids yesterday. She's been sleeping quite peacefully most of the day.

I finally got to experience kangaroo care with Amy in the evening. It was fantastic and she was very good. Having skin to skin contact with the girls is just the most wonderful experience.

Monday 15 June 1998

Hailey 935 grams / Amy 865 grams

Both girls have been putting on weight, which is great. Hailey has now reached two pounds one ounce and Amy is not far behind.

Amy's oxygen has been hovering around 35-40%, sometimes lower, which is good. She is becoming very active and likes to hold her tubes for security and comfort.

Hailey had eye drops put in this morning as they were going to check her eyes. She must have known, because she had a long desaturation, so they will do the eye test next week. The eye test is quite uncomfortable for them, so it's best to wait until she's a bit bigger. Her feeds have started to be fortified so I hope she can cope with it.

I did kangaroo care with Hailey, which was lovely. She slept beautifully and it made me feel great. I also did kangaroo care with Amy, which was also lovely. She was very happy and went into air for a bit.

What a wonderful day I had, being able to do kangaroo care with both my daughters.

Tuesday 16 June 1998 (6 weeks old)

Hailey is the same as yesterday. She had a blood test today to check her levels for different things.

Amy has made me age ten years today. She had two A2's, which basically means she forgot to breathe. The nurses were very quick to act and worked on her straight away. She has had a chest X-ray done to check the position of her tube and her lungs. The tube needed to be put down about half a centimetre. Her lungs are still the same as a couple of days ago.

Her feeding tube has been moved to her mouth, freeing her nostril for breathing. Amy has been put on an iron supplement to help her development also. She was in air during the evening when we were with her, which was good.

It has been found that Amy has an infection, which would have triggered her earlier episodes. They are not going to treat it at this stage, just keep a close eye on her. Her feeds have been increased to 5.5 ml hourly. It looks like a long, slow road for my precious Amy, but I'm patient.

Hailey is getting up to mischief herself. Tonight she had her finger in her nose. We've put a dummy in her cot, and if she becomes unsettled overnight, the nurse will try her with the dummy. She has been sneezing, which is so cute and it's helping keep her secretions to a minimum.

Wednesday 17 June 1998

Hailey 1,001 grams / Amy 888 grams

Amy is better today than she was yesterday. They are still not treating her infection, in the hope it will only take a couple of days to go. I feel satisfied that at least we have a reason for what happened yesterday.

Hailey was a bit naughty overnight. She had a few desaturations so the doctors have said that if it continues she will need to go back on the prong. At least it's not stopping her from putting on weight, as she has now reached over 1000 grams (1 kilo). Amy is not too far behind.

We tried both girls on dummies today. Amy appeared to like it but didn't have the ability to hold it in. It did pacify her though. Hailey just spat the dummy out straight away; she obviously didn't like it.

Thursday 18 June 1998

Hailey had more desaturations last night and her oxygen requirements went quite high. The doctors are concerned that perhaps she's getting tired, so she will probably go on the CPAP driver for a couple of days to help her. Her feeds have been increased to 6.5 ml hourly.

I tried Hailey with a dummy again today and this time she appeared to like it. She managed to hold it in place herself – what a clever girl.

Amy had a pretty good night. Her ventilator has been turned down to 20 and her oxygen is around 30%.

Hailey is much better during the day and plays up at night, whereas Amy is better at night and plays up during the day. It looks like I'm in for some fun times.

In the afternoon, Hailey was put on the CPAP driver. It has two small nose prongs held in place with a 'fashionable' hat. It pushes air into her lungs, helping keep them open and making it easier for her to breathe. She did fantastic breathing on her own for thirteen days and has just got a bit tired.

Friday 19 June 1998

Hailey 1,042 grams / Amy 883 grams

Amy has had the long tube taken out and the nasal prong put in. It means she has to work harder and breathe for herself. She has done well and been in air most of the day. I hope she can manage on her own with the nasal prong, but if not, we'll try again another day. So far so good though. The head doctor even commented that Amy is doing well, which is encouraging.

Hailey is still resting on the driver and her saturation has been better. She has been in air, not requiring oxygen.

Saturday 20 June 1998

Hailey had a try off the driver this morning. She did well and was off for about two and half hours in air. It must be uncomfortable for her, considering that for thirteen days she breathed on her own and now she is back on assistance. It's better however for her, because she needed the rest and was requiring a bit of oxygen.

They are aiming to get her off the driver into air without requiring oxygen at all. I think it could be a bit of time for this to happen. It doesn't appear to be bothering her; she is still being herself. Her feeds have been increased to 7 ml hourly.

I had a kangaroo cuddle with Hailey today, which was wonderful.

Amy has still been excellent with the nasal prong and hasn't required any oxygen. When she is awake, she is becoming agitated and tries to wriggle away from the tube in her nose. I watch her and panic that she might hurt herself. Towards the end of the day, she was requiring a bit of oxygen, so I hope she is not tiring and heading back again to the long tube.

Sunday 21 June 1998
Hailey 1,090 grams / Amy 894 grams

Amy is still quite restless when she wakes up. She likes the dummy and sucks it quite vigorously. If she's awake, the nurses give her the dummy when she has her feed, to give her the sensation of her tummy filling whilst sucking the dummy (helps for when we try breastfeeding).

They changed her nasal prong today so I saw her beautiful face again without tubes and tape. She has lovely big cheeks and gorgeous lips. I know both girls will be heartbreakers when they're older.

Hailey is coming off the driver for two to four hours every eight. Her right nostril is quite traumatised, so they want to give her nose a rest. When she is on the driver she is usually in air, but when she's off she is requiring minimum cot oxygen. Her feeds have been reduced to 6 ml hourly, because this morning her abdomen was quite swollen. She has since done two big poos, so they will review her feeds again.

Hailey now outweighs Amy by about 200 grams, so I hope Amy catches up soon.

I had a lovely kangaroo cuddle with Amy in the afternoon.

I'm feeling a lot of frustration at the moment. The girls are doing well but I wish the process was quicker.

Monday 22 June 1998

Hailey has still been having periods off the driver, but each time she is requiring cot oxygen. She has also been requiring a small amount of oxygen at times when the driver is on. It is certainly noticeable that Hailey is putting on weight and growing in length.

Amy's oxygen requirements have been creeping up. Her respiratory rate has been good, which means her breathing is fine. She is having build-ups of secretions behind the tube. They would like to change her over to the CPAP driver as soon as one becomes available.

I had a lovely cuddle with Hailey in the afternoon.

Tuesday 23 June 1998 (7 weeks old)
Hailey 1,085 grams / 919 grams

Amy has had a peaceful day with plenty of sleep. She has been requiring oxygen throughout most of the day. We are still waiting for a driver to be available for her. The nurses believe this would help her a lot and reduce oxygen requirements. Amy had a top-up of blood overnight.

Hailey had a bit of a distended tummy overnight as she hadn't done a poo for a few days, however she did later in the morning. They have stopped putting fortifier in her feeds, as this thickens the milk and makes it a bit harder to pass through the system. They will review it again once she starts doing regular poos.

I had a nice cuddle with Hailey in the afternoon for two hours whilst she was off the driver.

Hailey is having a top-up of blood overnight because her haemoglobin is low.

I had a brief but beautiful kangaroo cuddle with Amy in the evening.

Wednesday 24 June 1998

Hailey is still good and looks very pretty in a dress today. Her feeds have been increased to 7 ml hourly, and if she tolerates that well, it will probably have fortifier added to it again from tomorrow.

Amy has made a step forward and is now on the CPAP driver. Her desaturations have decreased since she went on the driver at about 9 am this morning. She has been requiring a bit of oxygen but this is okay.

She has been sleeping quite peacefully, so hopefully now that the nasal tube has gone she will be able to get required oxygen through to her lungs better. She was getting a lot of secretion build-up behind the tube, so at least this will be avoided now.

I had a nice cuddle with Hailey in the evening. I wish I could hold Amy as often as I'm holding Hailey. Once Amy's oxygen requirements have settled, hopefully I will be able to.

Thursday 25 June 1998
Hailey 1,090 grams / Amy 939 grams

Amy's oxygen requirements have still been up and down, although much better since she's been on the driver. She had a cry when I was with her in the evening. It breaks my heart hearing her cry, because I know something is bothering or hurting her, however I do love the sound of her voice. Once she had some milk she settled, so perhaps she was hungry.

I gave Hailey a sponge bath and weigh in the morning, which was lovely. She was disconnected from all her leads and her feeding tube was out, so it made it much easier. Her cot temperature has been turned down so she can have clothes put on and not overheat. I had a lovely hold of Hailey in the morning and evening.

Friday 26 June 1998

Hailey's milk has recommenced having fortifier added to it. Hopefully she will put on weight at a quicker pace, rather than the slow pace of the last few days. She's still having time off the driver, up to four hours every eight hour shift, which she enjoys.

It was a special day for Amy; she was dressed for the first time in a pretty white with pink flowers dress. She came off the driver for about nine hours during the day, which was great because it gave her nose and face a rest. She required cot and head box oxygen, which is oxygen administered directly into the Isolette while the head box is placed over her to give her warm and humidified oxygen to breathe in. She looked so happy and peaceful when she slept.

Amy's steroids have been stopped, and if she continues going well with her breathing and minimal secretions, her physio will be stopped tomorrow. I feel very happy that Amy is getting better and stronger each day. Hopefully soon she will be able to move up with Hailey to Bay 5.

I had another special cuddle with Hailey in the afternoon. I can't wait till Amy's well and truly stable and I can have a long lovely cuddle with her.

I love both the girls so much. I never knew such strong emotions existed.

Saturday 27 June 1998

Hailey 1,150 grams / Amy 947 grams

I had another special day today. I gave both Hailey and Amy a wash and they smelt and looked nice and clean. I also had a long-awaited cuddle with Amy which made me very happy.

Amy is still doing well on the driver. She is requiring minimal amounts of oxygen. Her physio has been stopped so this is a good indication that she is on the improve.

Hailey is getting stronger each time she is off the driver. She starts off in air, and towards the end of her four hours off is requiring minimal oxygen. She certainly looks more peaceful and relaxed when she is off the driver.

Sunday 28 June 1998

Hailey was off the driver all night because she had quite a traumatised nose. She went back on mid-morning and has been sleeping peacefully since.

Amy is still getting grisly at times. She certainly enjoys the dummy and settles quite well once it's given to her. She tries to hold it in herself and gets frustrated when it falls out.

I'm feeling very frustrated at the moment too. Both girls are doing well and progressing with their breathing, but it's a waiting game for them to grow and stop requiring oxygen, etc. I'm looking forward to giving them their first bath (at 1,500 grams), trying breastfeeding and being able to cuddle them without asking permission.

I've always been an impatient person and I'm finding it difficult because I have to be patient. I know Hailey and Amy are doing the best they can, and I love them even more for it.

Amy had a break off the driver in the afternoon so I was able to give her a lovely cuddle without any tubes on her face. She was very happy and slept beautifully.

Amy is ready to move from Bay 6 to Bay 5, but we have to wait for a baby to move from Bay 5 to make room for her. It would be lovely to have the girls together in the same room again.

I had a lovely cuddle with Hailey in the evening, and then did something even more special, I carried Hailey from Bay 5 to Bay 6 for Hailey and Amy to see each other. Unfortunately, they were both asleep, but it was nice for us to look at them together.

Monday 29 June 1998

Hailey 1,210 grams / Amy 990 grams

Amy is now having one hour off the driver every eight. This will be good to give her nose a break and also a rest from the equipment. Her feeds are being increased to 6.5 ml hourly from midnight. I had a lovely cuddle with Amy in the afternoon.

Hailey's getting stronger each time she is off the driver. She is now four hours on and four hours off; if she's doing well she will be left off longer. They are trying to keep her in air when she is off the driver – so far, so good. Her feeds have been increased to 7.5 ml hourly. I gave Hailey a wash and a cuddle in the morning.

It's so much nicer holding the girls when they are off the driver. I can bring them closer to me without the intrusion of tubes.

Tuesday 30 June 1998 (8 weeks old)

Hailey is looking a bit puffy, so she has been put on a diuretic drug. This will help her wee more and reduce the puffiness. She is still in air most of the time when she is off the driver. She has been getting quite a few secretions and this is affecting her breathing and oxygen requirements when off the driver.

Amy is now off the driver for up to two hours every eight hours. She still requires oxygen, but this is not a problem at this stage. She has been desaturating more when she is having her milk so she may need to start Cisapride to help her digest the feed better.

I had a lovely kangaroo cuddle with Hailey in the evening. When she first was with me she was wide awake and playing with my necklace, then she went into a peaceful sleep.

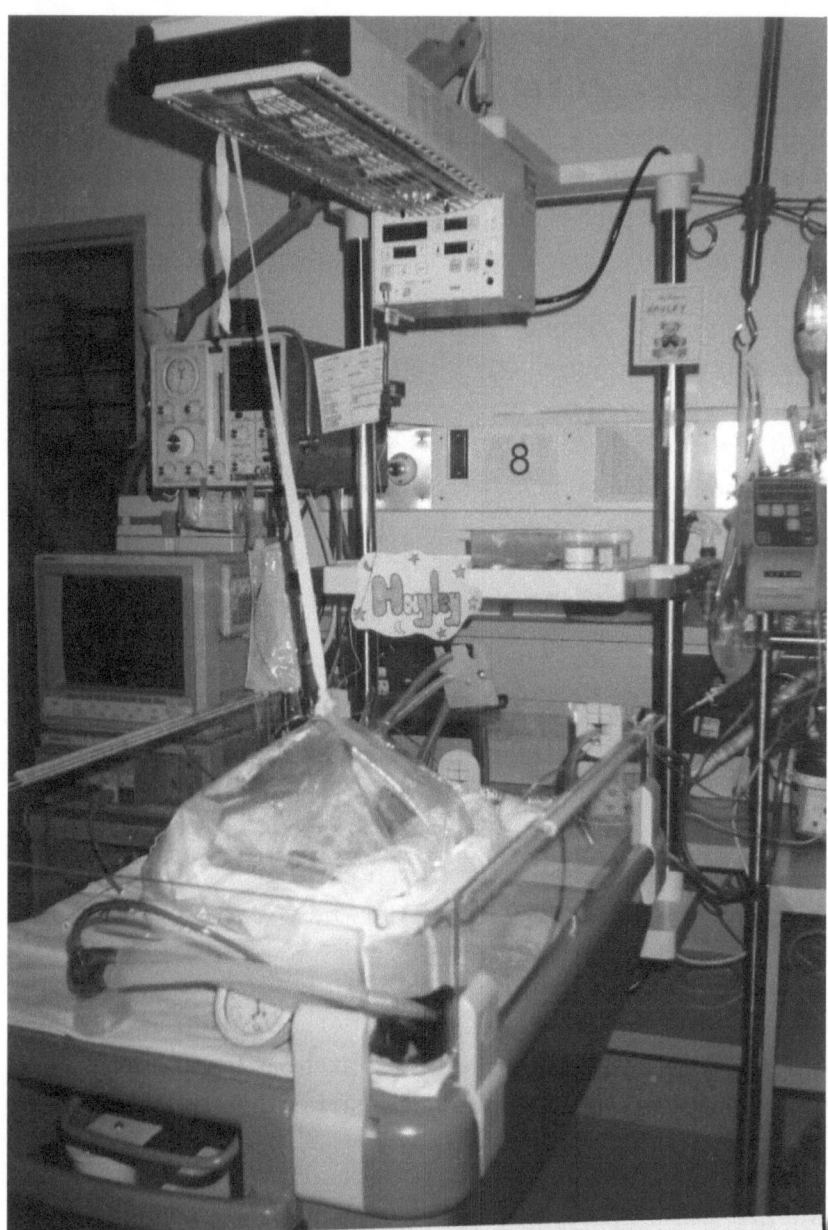

6 May 1998. Hailey, one day old, protected by a 'plastic bag' to keep her body temperature regular. Her ventilator tubes are going into the bag through a small hole at the top.

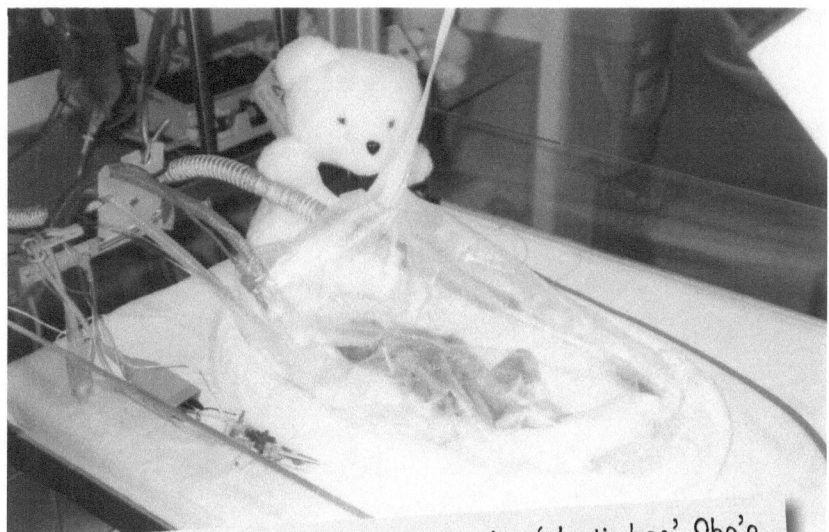

11 May 1998. Amy, six days old, in her 'plastic bag'. She's being watched over by her first special teddy bear.

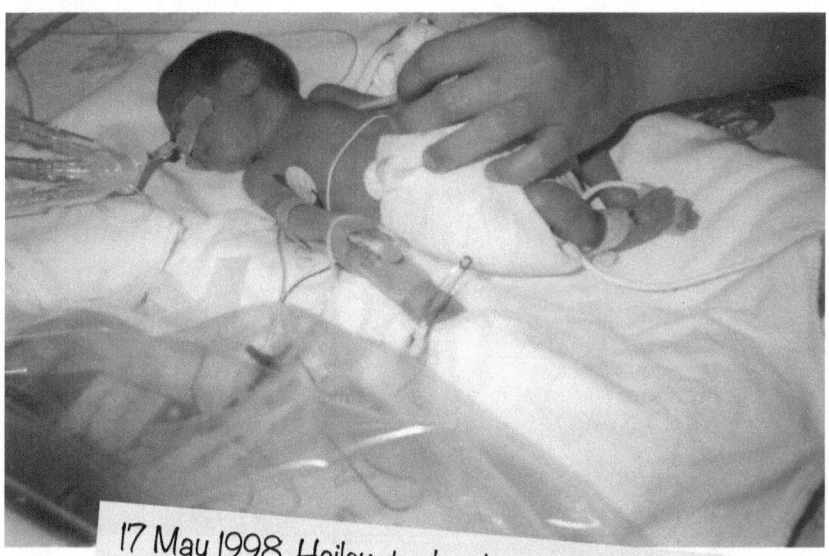

17 May 1998. Hailey, twelve days old, sleeping peacefully while her nurse checks her monitors.

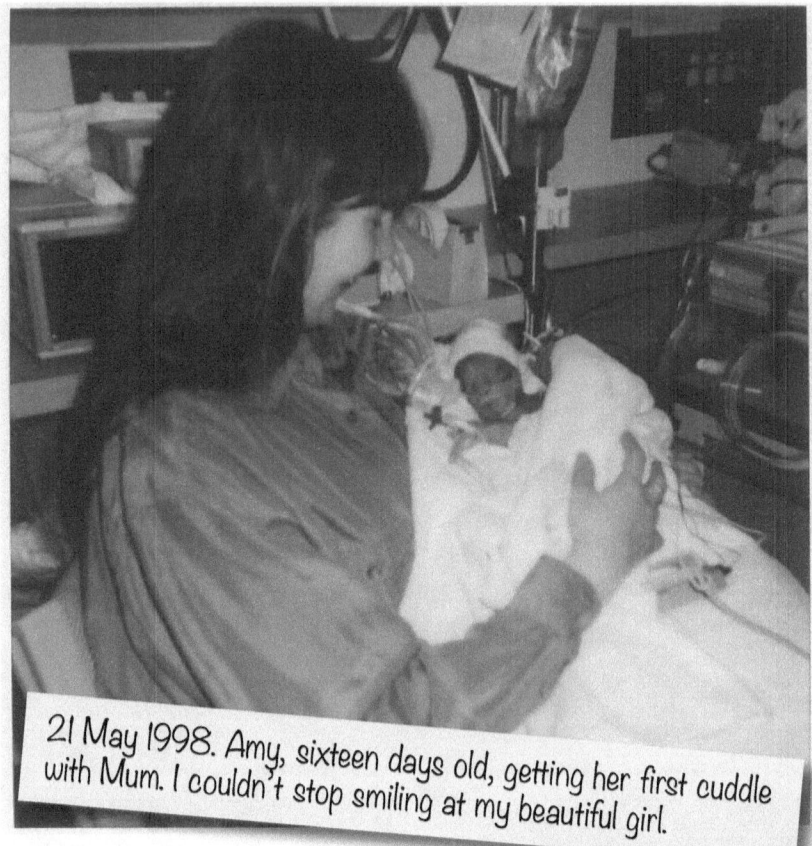

21 May 1998. Amy, sixteen days old, getting her first cuddle with Mum. I couldn't stop smiling at my beautiful girl.

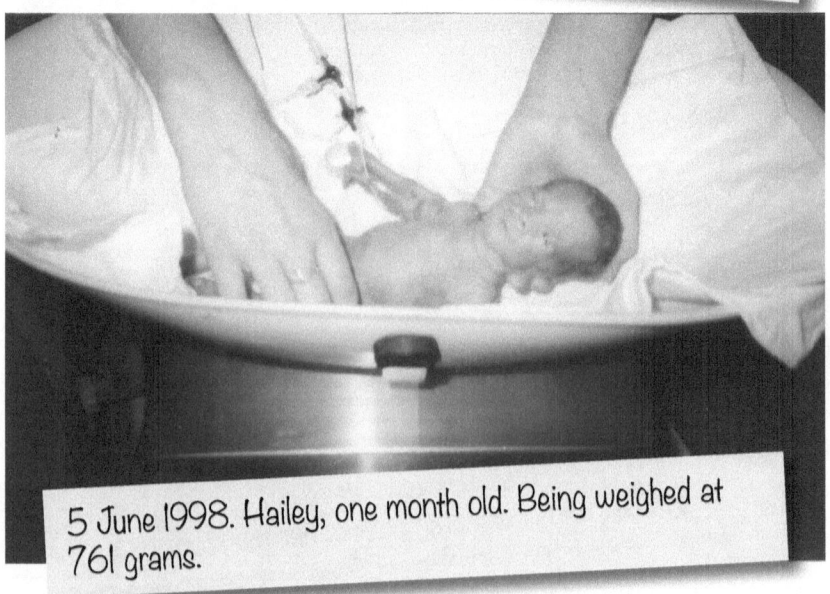

5 June 1998. Hailey, one month old. Being weighed at 761 grams.

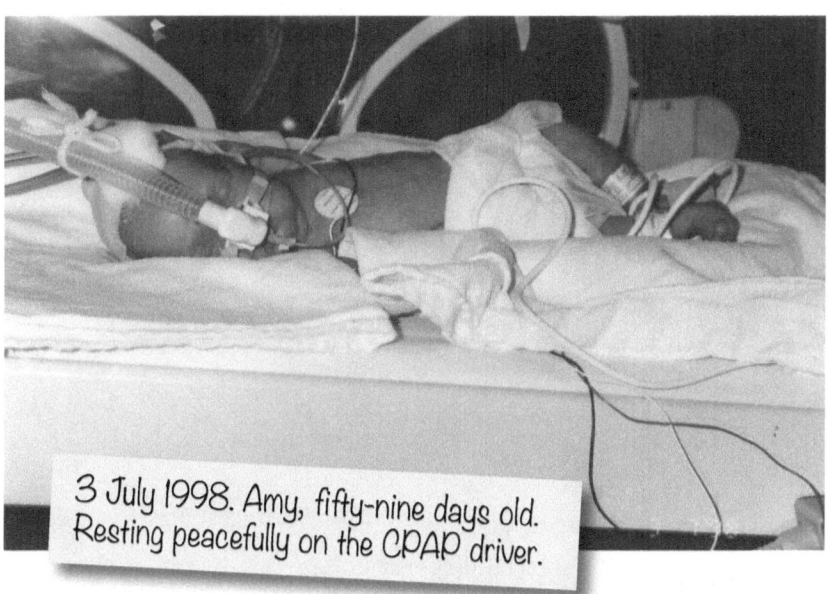

3 July 1998. Amy, fifty-nine days old. Resting peacefully on the CPAP driver.

26 July 1998. Amy and Hailey at eighty-two days old. One of my happiest days of their hospital stay – the first time I was able to hold them together.

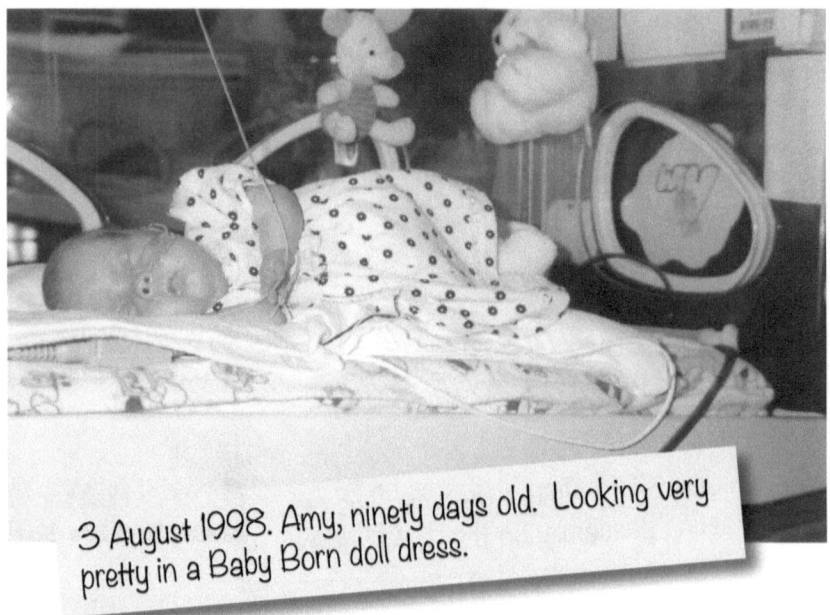

3 August 1998. Amy, ninety days old. Looking very pretty in a Baby Born doll dress.

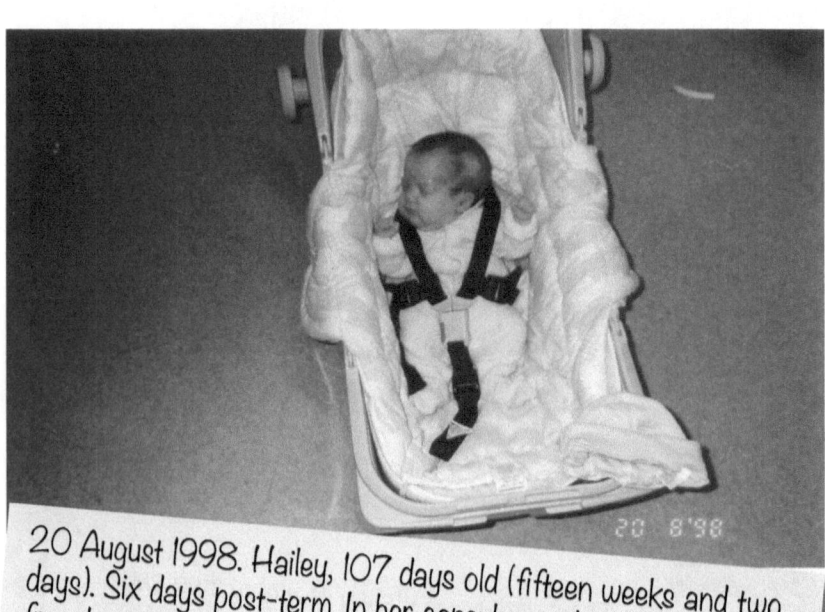

20 August 1998. Hailey, 107 days old (fifteen weeks and two days). Six days post-term. In her capsule, ready to go home from hospital.

Hailey and Amy

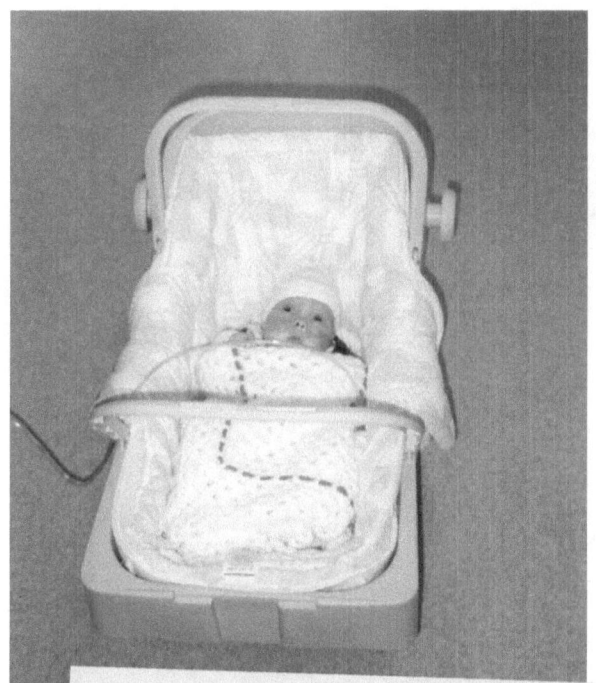

15 September 1998. Amy, 133 days old (nineteen weeks) Thirty-two days post-term. In her capsule, ready to go home from hospital, connected to oxygen.

27 April 1999. A week before they turned one. Hailey and Amy having a play and laugh together at home.

13 August 2001. Hailey and Amy, three years old. Having fun playing together at playgroup.

2 August 2003. Hailey and Amy, five years old. This has always been a favourite photo of the girls, dressed as Cinderella and Sleeping Beauty for a fairytale party.

4 December 2008. Hailey and Amy, ten years old. Writing letters to Santa at Santa's Cave.

21 August 2011. Hailey and Amy, thirteen years old. Enjoying a relaxing picnic at Lillydale Lake.

A Mother's Love for Her Miracle Twins

20 March 2015. Amy and Hailey, sixteen years old. Arriving at their Year 11 school formal.

4 December 2016. Hailey and Amy, eighteen years old. At North Coast Regional Botanic Gardens, Coffs Harbour during their end of Year 12 trip.

A Mother's Love for Her Miracle Twins

Front page of Knox News Tuesday 3 November 1998. At the time of Hailey and Amy's birth, it is believed they were the smallest surviving twins Monash Medical Centre had cared for.

Knox News

▲ 1.7 million people read a local *Leader* newspaper every week

Classifieds 9875 8200   Inquiries 9762 2511   TUESDAY, NOVEMBER 3, 1998   19 Chandler Road, Boronia   40c

Proud parents: Narelle and Brad Docking hold their twins Amy and Hailey, "going from strength to strength". Picture: JASON SAMMON

'Miracle' twins

Hospital battle over

by SARAH DAWSON

BRAD DOCKING couldn't believe his ears when he received a 'phone call telling him his wife was about to give birth to their IVF twins 15 weeks early.

Almost six months later, after beating odds of 60 to 70 per cent chance of survival, Brad and his wife Narelle, of Knoxfield, are enjoying life at home with their babies.

"We call Hailey our miracle and Amy our battler," Mrs Docking said.

"The staff at Monash Medical Centre are so dedicated to enable our babies to survive."

Hailey has come through a traumatic start to life with no long-term effects. Amy almost had to have eye surgery and she is on oxygen 24-hours a day until at least Christmas because of poorly formed lungs.

"They're going from strength-to-strength each week," Mrs Docking said.

"It's amazing what they've gone through."

Back in April, Narelle Docking was at work when her waters broke 24 weeks into her pregnancy.

She drove herself to Waverley Private Hospital and was then rushed to Monash Medical Centre in Clayton.

A week later, after developing an infection, Narelle had an emergency caesarean.

The two girls were born on May 5. Hailey weighed a mere 670gm and Amy just 592gm.

Hailey spent five weeks in intensive care and Amy nine weeks. In total, Hailey spent 107 days at Monash Medical Centre and Amy 133 days.

For Narelle her life centred around sitting by her babies' hospital cribs.

"I'd get in about 10.30am every day and come home for tea then go back until 11pm," she said.

"Basically I'd be home to eat and sleep.

"It was very tiring emotionally. I didn't think I was ever going to see the end. It seemed like an eternity.

"I feel like I lost four and half months this year."

Now Amy weighs 3020gm or six pounds 10 ounces and Hailey 3250gm or seven pounds 2 1/2 ounces — the size of newborns.

"They're almost six months old, but only 10 weeks in corrected age," Mrs Docking said.

"By the time they get to school they will have caught up in size with children their age."

Article in Knox News – Tuesday 18 May 1999
A follow-up story just after the girls turned one.

Tiny twins celebrate their first birthday

Miracle milestone: *premature twins Amy and Hailey Docking celebrate their first birthday with parents Narelle and Brad.*

JUST over a year ago, Narelle Docking gave birth to IVF twins 15 weeks early.

Hailey was born weighing only 670 grams and her sister Amy only 592 grams (about the size of a tub of margarine). At three months of age Amy was so tiny she was still wearing doll's clothes.

Last week parents Narelle and Brad, of Knoxfield, were thrilled to see the twins reach what was probably their most important milestone — their first birthday.

"It was something I really didn't think we'd get to. I couldn't foresee getting to 12 months," Mrs Docking said.

"I look back this time 12 months ago — you see these tiny little babies in plastic bags and IV machines all over them . . ."

The two girls were born on May 5 last year at the Monash Medical Centre. Hailey spent five weeks in intensive care and Amy nine weeks. Mrs Docking was not even able to touch Amy until five days after she was born.

Mr Docking said they were just like "little skeletons" while they were in the humidicrib.

"Those four-and-a-half months in the hospital were an eternity," Mrs Docking said. "I slept through pure exhaustion."

Amy has chronic lung disease, and depended on oxygen 24 hours a day until late February this year.

The girls are now much healthier, although Amy only weighs 5880gm and Hailey 7650gm.

Month 3

July 1998

Wednesday 1 July 1998

Hailey 1,235 grams / Amy 1,040 grams

Amy has finally hit the 1,000 grams. I'm very proud of her progress. She is now off the driver for up to three hours every eight which is excellent. She is becoming aware of when her feed is due and will sometimes wake up and cry until she is fed.

We're going to try Hailey on the breast at the end of the week. I don't think she'll be very interested, but it's worth a try. I feel Amy will take to breastfeeding before Hailey. Amy loves sucking on the dummy and if you put something near her mouth she will open it and run her tongue around it.

I gave Hailey a wash and a cuddle in the morning, which was lovely. Her feeds have been increased to 8 ml hourly and she is off the driver for up to six hours every eight.

I have noticed over the past couple of days that the girls' eyes are now wide open and they appear to be more alert.

Thursday 2 July 1998

Hailey appears to be getting stronger each day. Most of the time now when she is off the driver she is in air, and when she is on the driver, she is in air all the time. She can now be left off the driver for as long as she tolerates. I had a nice cuddle with Hailey in the afternoon.

Amy is now on 7 ml of milk every hour. She is off the driver for up to four hours every eight and is also looking stronger every day.

At the moment Hailey has the more placid temperament and isn't fazed by being touched. Amy appears to want more attention and cries if she's awake and it's close to feed time. She wriggles around the cot and kicks her legs and waves her arms around and often needs a dummy to settle her.

Friday 3 July 1998

Hailey 1,211 grams / Amy 1,093 grams

Amy has been showing signs of getting tired when she is off the driver. They are keeping an eye on her and only taking her off if they feel she will cope. She is being started on diuretics to help flush through fluid on her lungs. I had a nice cuddle with Amy in the afternoon when she came off the driver.

Hailey is still off the driver (she came off about 8 am yesterday) and doing well. They will leave her off unless she has too many desaturations. She is in air and hasn't been requiring oxygen, which is good. Hailey's diuretics have been stopped.

We had a progress meeting with the doctors today. Hailey is medically doing well and now needs to fatten up and establish her feeding. They are pleased with her progress so far off the driver. There is a chance she may be ready to go home close to their due date, in six-weeks time.

The doctors are happy with Amy medically; they are just concerned about getting her off the driver and out of oxygen. The minimal oxygen she is requiring is not a concern however. As she grows, her lungs are growing. Amy will hopefully be ready to come home in six to ten weeks.

The only thing that could set the girls back is if they get an infection, so we have to do everything we can to avoid this. Overall the doctors are pleased with the progress of both girls.

Hailey and Amy had eye tests today to check the development of their eyes. Retinopathy of prematurity (ROP) is an eye disease that can occur in premature babies, and both girls need to be monitored for it. Hailey's eyes are scored as one on a scale of one to ten, with ten being severe underdevelopment. She will be checked again in about three weeks. Amy's eyes are a two/three and will be checked again next week.

It doesn't appear to be a concern with either girl, just something that needs to be monitored closely so any necessary action can be attended to straight away.

It was another special day for Hailey and me. We put her to the breast for the first time. She had a few sucks, quite a few licks and got some milk. She appeared to know what to do, just not the strength to do much. It was good for her first attempt. She was also given her usual amount of milk then proceeded to vomit on my chest – oh well, I didn't mind.

Saturday 4 July 1998

Hailey is still off the driver and in air. She has had a few desaturations but there hasn't been any talk of putting her back on the driver. She has been sleeping quite peacefully for most of the day.

Amy's time off the driver has been reduced to two to three hours, as she wasn't quite coping with four hours. Her feeds have been increased to 7.5 ml hourly. I had a lovely cuddle with Amy in the morning. She is quite restless at the moment when she is sleeping and when she's awake.

Sunday 5 July 1998
Hailey 1,270 grams / Amy 1,050 grams

Amy is still getting stronger each day. When she is on the driver, she is in air most of the time. Her time off the driver is now three hours, however she does require minimal oxygen when off the driver. I'm getting frustrated that she's still in Bay 6 when they keep telling me she's ready to move on.

Brad had a nice cuddle with Amy in the morning. Amy's breathing is getting much better and she really is progressing well.

Hailey is still doing very well. She has been off the driver since 8 am Thursday and has been coping really well. Her breathing has been good and only had a few desaturations. They have actually moved the driver machine away from her, so they must have confidence that she can cope on her own. Hailey's feeds are being increased to 9 ml hourly from midnight.

I'm very proud of both girls' progress. They are certainly showing signs of being very strong individuals.

We tried Hailey on the breast again in the afternoon and she responded well. I think we will try her every day or every second day. I also had a lovely cuddle with her.

I had a cuddle and kangaroo cuddle with Amy in the evening. She vomited on me and managed to squirm away from the vomit and fall asleep, leaving me with it sitting on my chest and in my bra.

Monday 6 July 1998

Hailey is tolerating her 9 ml of milk hourly. She is now on a drug called Fergon which is an iron supplement.

Today was a special day for Amy and me. When I arrived at the hospital in the morning, she was crying for food, so the nurse asked if I would like to try her on the breast. She was very good and latched herself on well, had a few sucks and got herself some milk. It was a nice experience for me and hopefully Amy. She has been vomiting a bit through the day, so I don't know if they might cut her feeds down.

Hailey has had a good day of sleeping and Amy has had a day of being awake and grisly – what a lovely pair they make.

Hailey wasn't as interested in the breast when we tried her in the evening. The nurse feels confident that she will get the hang of it in time. I also had a nice cuddle with Hailey in the evening.

Both girls appear to know what they have to do with breast feeding, they just need the strength and encouragement to put it into practice.

Tuesday 7 July 1998 (9 weeks old)
Hailey 1,375 grams / Amy 1,110 grams

What a wonderful day today was. Not only were the girls nine weeks old today, but Amy has been moved to Bay 5 next to Hailey (she is still a NICU baby though).

Amy appears happy in her new home. She has been started on the drug Cisapride, because it appears she has reflux and this should help her. The three hours off the driver have been tiring her out, so they will just see how long she lasts and sometimes put her back on after two hours.

Hailey has hit the three pound mark. She appears to have a bit of fluid retention though so they will keep an eye on her. They might start her on two hourly feeds soon. She was much better on the breast today.

I gave both girls a nice wash in the afternoon.

Wednesday 8 July 1998

Hailey was looking a bit puffy in the morning so she was given a one-off drug to help her wee out some retained fluid. Oh and did she wee – she saturated her nappy, clothes and bed linen. She was sounding a bit snuffly in the afternoon so I hope she isn't getting a cold; if so she may need to go back on the driver. Her feeds have been graded throughout the day on an hourly basis to build her up to two hourly feeds. That means she will be on 18 ml two hourly. If she tolerates it, great, if not she will go back to hourly feeds for now. I had a nice quick cuddle with Hailey in the afternoon.

Amy appears happy in her new Bay next to Hailey. She has had a peaceful sleeping day. I had a nice long cuddle with Amy in the afternoon. She was very relaxed with me and slept beautifully.

I'm trying to touch the girls in a soothing way and cuddle them as much as possible because I believe it helps comfort and stimulate them.

Thursday 9 July 1998

Hailey 1,409 grams

Amy didn't respond very well to being off the driver this morning; she had numerous desaturations. I hope she gets stronger soon. She had a follow-up eye check done and her eyes are about the same. Sometimes with the eye problem she has, it can get worse before it gets better. She will be given daily eye drops to keep her pupils dilated in the hope the condition does not get any worse.

I hope her eyes improve soon. Amy really has a lot to contend with.

Hailey has still been doing well and had minimal desaturations. She is now on 18 ml of milk two hourly which, so far, she has been tolerating quite well. I gave Hailey a wash and a cuddle in the afternoon. Hailey will be having a blood top-up overnight.

Had a lovely cuddle with Amy in the evening.

Friday 10 July 1998

Amy 1,156 grams

Hailey got quite sick overnight. Her feeds have been ceased and she is being fed by an IV drip. Her tummy became distended, so she had an abdominal X-ray done. This shows a build-up of gas and/or bile in her bowel. She has a tube through her mouth to her tummy to dispel the bile and is on antibiotics. She hasn't been herself for the past couple of days and this is why.

The surgeons will look at her this afternoon and give their opinion on what action to take. She has a cannula in one of her arms. I guess this is one of those setbacks we've often been told about. I hate seeing her unwell like this.

Amy is still not tolerating the time off the driver very well. She is having a top-up of blood tonight, so hopefully this will help her. Amy's feeds are now 8 ml hourly. I gave her a wash and a brief kangaroo cuddle in the afternoon.

Hailey did two big poos during the day. She appeared to be more herself during the afternoon, so hopefully she just has an infection (which is being treated by the antibiotics). The surgeon had a look at her tummy and wants another X-ray tomorrow. Hopefully the infection she has, has caused her bowel not to work properly and now she is on the mend.

Saturday 11 July 1998

Amy is having a day of rest; she will not be coming off the driver during the day. She was desaturating a lot in the morning until they discovered she had partly pulled her feeding tube out. Her Cisapride has been stopped for now.

Hailey is much better today. She is a lot more active. She is still on antibiotics and IV feeds though. The doctors feel that perhaps her bowel build-up was due to an infection. They will do another abdominal X-ray tomorrow but they are pretty certain her system is fine. Her tummy is having a rest today and hopefully feeds will start again tomorrow which will make her happy.

I had a lovely kangaroo cuddle with Hailey in the afternoon.

Amy's tummy became quite distended in the afternoon and she was desaturating a bit. Her feeds have been reduced to 4 ml hourly of unfortified milk and 4 ml hourly of IV feeds. She is also having a blood test to check for infection. Amy has an IV cannula in her arm like Hailey.

Sunday 12 July 1998

Amy is better today than she was yesterday afternoon. She had a chest and abdomen X-ray done in the morning which were fine. There is no sign of infection and her tummy has gone down. Her feeds are being increased during the day, so by midnight she will be back on full feeds and the IV drip can be removed. Her milk will remain unfortified for now. She has been desaturating quite a bit, so they are going to leave her in a bit of oxygen and keep her on the driver all day. She appears to be resting quite well.

Amy's need for oxygen assistance is due to her having Chronic Lung Disease (CLD). I hope she gets strong enough soon so she no longer requires any oxygen.

Hailey is getting better each day. She has had the tube removed from her tummy, and if she doesn't vomit she will be started back on feeds tonight or tomorrow morning. She is very active and appears to be getting frustrated that she hasn't had any milk for a couple of days. They will not be doing a follow-up X-ray at this stage, but will keep a close eye on her tummy. It appears she got an infection which caused her tummy not to tolerate or dispel her feeds. Because she was unable to tell us she wasn't well, her tummy got quite infected and distended before action was taken.

Monday 13 July 1998
Hailey 1,410 grams / Amy 1,279 grams

Hailey is finally starting back on feeds today. They are going to take it slowly, so she is starting on 1 ml four hourly and then it will gradually go up. She is definitely feeling better and hasn't had any desaturations for a while now. I gave Hailey a wash and we had a nice cuddle in the afternoon.

Amy is still up and down with oxygen requirements. She has had her IV removed and is back on full milk feeds which is good. They are commencing cycling her off the driver again, just one hour every eight to start. Amy had a wash and a nice but quick cuddle in the morning. You can definitely see that Amy has put on quite a lot of weight.

Tuesday 14 July 1998

Amy is being cycled off the driver two hours every eight if she tolerates it. Her feeds are still 7 ml hourly and not fortified. She is still requiring oxygen, on and off the driver. I had a lovely cuddle with Amy in the morning.

Hailey is improving every day. She is still on the IV drip for glucose, and her feeds are now 1 ml of milk every two hours. It is going to be a slow process getting her feeds back to what they were before she got sick (18 ml every two hours). She will be on hourly feeds before going back to two hourly feeds.

Wednesday 15 July 1998

Hailey 1,440 grams / Amy 1,325 grams

Amy is having another blood top-up today. She is also being put back on diuretics because she is looking a bit puffy. Her feeds are still 7 ml hourly and are being fortified again.

Hailey's feeds are now 1 ml of milk hourly. She is still being very active and I'm sure she finds having the IV in her arm most annoying.

Amy had a very quick bath today which she didn't protest about, then we had a short but nice cuddle.

Hailey also had a quick bath and appeared to enjoy it. I had a nice kangaroo cuddle with Hailey in the afternoon.

Thursday 16 July 1998

Hailey's feeds are being graded up 1 ml hourly every 12 hours. By the end of the weekend she should be back to 9 ml hourly if she tolerates it. Hailey is having a nightly enema to help flush out her bowels. She is still on antibiotics.

Amy's feeds are now back to 8 ml hourly of fortified milk. She is in air most of the time when she is on the driver, but not coping very well when she is off, often requiring up to 30% oxygen.

I had a nice cuddle with Hailey in the afternoon. Hailey's IV is now in her leg. Her veins are very sensitive so it's making it difficult for them to put the IV in. If this one in her leg packs up, the only place left to put one is through her head.

Friday 17 July 1998
Amy 1,258 grams

Amy is showing signs of improvement with her breathing and saturations over the last day or so. She is now off the driver three hours every eight, and has been requiring only minimal oxygen. The diuretics have helped get rid of retained fluid and even her cheeks are looking less chubby. Her hair is growing and remaining a nice honey blonde colour. I gave Amy a wash and cuddle in the afternoon.

Hailey's infection appears to have cleared, so hopefully the antibiotics will be stopped today. Her feeds are now being increased 1 ml every hour to get her back to full feeds quicker. As soon as this occurs and she's tolerating it, they will take the IV out of her leg. She really is very strong to have been so sick and get better in a week without requiring oxygen assistance or ventilation.

Saturday 18 July 1998
Hailey 1,535 grams

Today was another special day. Hailey had her first proper bath, and Brad and I had cuddles with the girls at the same time. Brad cuddled Hailey and I cuddled Amy. It was very special; the first time we have sat together as a family.

Hailey's antibiotics have been stopped and the IV removed. She is back on full milk feeds of 9 ml hourly, which is great. She is looking well and still very active. She certainly enjoyed her first bath, even though I was very nervous and scared I was going to drop her right in the water. She has been having a few desaturations today.

Amy is still cycling off the driver. When she first comes off, she breathes quite well, but by the end of the three hours she is having quite a few desaturations. I'm sure she will do it in her own time. The main thing is the bigger she grows, the bigger her lungs grow and the stronger she becomes.

Sunday 19 July 1998
Amy 1,303 grams

Amy is still improving each day on and off the driver. She is still three hours off and five hours on, but tomorrow it will be four on and four off the driver. Her salt medication has been reduced.

Hailey's desaturations have slowed down. If they increase, the doctors will consider putting her back on Theophylline, but at this stage, the less drugs the girls are on the better. Both girls need to be weaned off all drugs (except Cisapride for reflux) before they come home, so the earlier they stop the drugs the better as well.

I gave Amy a wash and then we had a nice long cuddle in the afternoon.

Amy's eyes were checked today and they are a bit worse. She needs to be seen by the professor this week. They still have time before any surgical treatment should begin. She is on daily eye drops now in the hope the retina will develop normally.

Monday 20 July 1998
Hailey 1,535 grams

Hailey's feeds have been increased to 10 ml hourly and she is also being graded up to two hourly feeds again. She is still having a few desaturations, but nothing to be concerned about at this stage.

Amy has a lot of secretions in her nose so they are going to check for infection. If she tolerates it, she will be off the driver for four hours and on for four. I'm feeling very concerned about her eyes. I hope the eyedrops work and her eyes don't get any worse.

Amy and I had a nice kangaroo cuddle in the afternoon.

I gave Hailey a bath in the afternoon which she enjoyed, and I felt a bit more confident in giving it to her.

Tuesday 21 July 1998

Amy 1,364 grams

Amy has hit three pounds. She is tolerating her four hours off the driver quite well, requiring between 25-30% cot oxygen. She is getting quite chubby and her hair is now looking strawberry blonde.

Hailey is tolerating her feeds of 20 ml two hourly well, and the milk is now being fortified so hopefully she will put on some weight. She is still having a few desaturations, down to about 85.

I had a kangaroo cuddle with Hailey in the morning and then had a nice cuddle with Amy in the evening.

Wednesday 22 July 1998

Hailey 1,563 grams

Hailey had another bath today, which I enjoyed giving her. It makes me feel good to be able to give the girls a bath. Hopefully Amy will be able to have one soon. I had a nice cuddle with Hailey in the afternoon.

Amy is now up to five hours off the driver and three on. I hope she responds well – so far so good. I had a nice cuddle with Amy in the morning. Amy is having a blood top-up tonight.

Thursday 23 July 1998

Amy 1,426 grams

Amy is continuing to do well. She is now cycling six hours off the driver and two on. Her eyes were checked again today and they are about the same as Sunday, but the professor will look at her tomorrow. At this stage they still feel no treatment (other than eye drops twice daily) is necessary.

Retinopathy of Prematurity (ROP) usually peaks around thirty-five to thirty-eight weeks gestation, then improves itself. Hopefully this will be Amy's case. Her feeds are now 8.5 ml hourly.

Amy's tummy got a bit distended in the afternoon so she was given an enema to help her poo. I hope she is just constipated and does not have the same infection Hailey had.

Hailey has had another turn backwards. The infection she had last week appears to have resurfaced. Her tummy is inflamed so she is back on antibiotics and IV drip for feeds. She will be kept off feeds for seven full days, then milk will be slowly introduced again. She has IVs in both her legs.

She has slept most of the day and been quite lethargic when she was awake. She had a blood top-up in the morning. Hailey's eyes were also checked today and there is still no problems with her retinas, so hopefully they will stay that way. She will be checked again in a couple of weeks.

Friday 24 July 1998

It's been found that Hailey has an infection in her blood (GBS – Group B Strep). They are not sure how she got it, because it usually only occurs shortly after birth, so are investigating it quite thoroughly. She is on Penicillin as well as antibiotics. Apparently Amy had the same infection when she was three weeks old.

Hailey has slept most of the day. I think she is feeling quite restricted with splints on her legs, because when she does wake up she often cries. She is still 'nil orally'. Her hair looks like it's going a lighter brown colour.

Amy had a good night. She was off the driver until about 9 am this morning, so she was off for about twenty-four hours. She was put back on for two hours, then taken off again. I'm not sure if they will cycle six hours off or what – we'll wait and see. She's been doing well though off the driver and in air most of the time.

Amy's feeds have been only 6 ml today with no fortifier due to her tummy distension yesterday afternoon. She had blood tests for infection and these were negative and her tummy appears to be fine today.

Amy's eyes were checked by the professor and he advised that they weren't as bad as what he expected them to be. He is happy to continue with eye drops and feels that no further treatment is necessary at this stage. They will check her eyes weekly and hopefully they should get better from now. At this stage they can't predict what, if any, vision problems will occur.

I had a cuddle and a kangaroo cuddle with Amy today.

Saturday 25 July 1998

Amy 1,459 grams

Amy is cycling off the driver, six hours off and two on. She has been doing well and is only requiring minimal oxygen off the driver. She should grow out of her oxygen dependency before she comes home. Her feeds have been increased to 7.5 ml hourly with no fortifier. I had a nice cuddle with Amy in the afternoon after I gave her a wash.

Hailey looks well and is quite active considering she has an infection. They are keeping two IV lines in her and are having trouble with her veins because they are so delicate. She has been crying a bit and is being comforted by sucking the dummy. I wish I could cuddle her and let her know everything will be okay. Hailey hasn't had any desaturations for a few days now.

Sunday 26 July 1998

Hailey 1,777 grams

Hailey has slept most of the day, which is good. She looks so peaceful when she sleeps, and quite frustrated when she is awake, because of the IVs in her and no food in her tummy. She is still on two antibiotics and Penicillin.

Amy is getting her breathing well and truly underway. Hopefully she will be off the driver for good in a couple of days. Her feeds are remaining at 7.5 ml hourly for now, to give her a chance to concentrate on breathing and not pushing her digestive system at the same time.

The love I have for the girls continues to grow stronger every day. I hate being away from them; I feel like part of me is missing when I am.

Amy has now found her voice and often cries when she is waking up or when she wants the driver machine off.

I had the most fantastic experience in the evening – a kangaroo cuddle with Hailey and Amy together. They gave each other a bit of a nudge, then Amy lay there looking at Hailey and Hailey was watching me. What a lovely time we had together.

Monday 27 July 1998
Amy 1,450 grams

Amy is now cycling seven hours off the driver and one on. Hopefully tomorrow she will come off for good. She will need cot oxygen for a little while though. I gave Amy a wash and a cuddle and she had another try at breastfeeding today. She did really well and got more milk than we'd thought. Amy is being tested for Group B Strep because Hailey has it and they want to make sure Amy isn't affected as well.

Hailey is still very restless when she is awake. I think she's really missing her milk and having something in her tummy. She is enjoying the dummy and sucks on it quite vigorously. They are still progressing with Hailey's treatment, and are at a loss to explain how she got Group B Strep when it usually only occurs either at or shortly after birth.

There are so many things happening each day that it is difficult to keep up with it all. I have done my best to note down as much as possible, but I'm sure I've missed things.

Tuesday 28 July 1998

Hailey has had to have an IV put in her forehead because the veins in her limbs are becoming very delicate. She still has an IV in her leg. They are talking about putting a long line in (a tube through a vein in her head to near her heart), which would last longer and avoid having to re-site two IVs every day.

The doctor was talking about putting Hailey in an open cot once all her IVs are out, probably in a couple of weeks. She will be on antibiotics for two more weeks and probably off all feeds for ten days before they slowly grade her back on to milk.

Amy has put her foot down. When they tried to put her on the driver in the early hours of the morning, she protested so much that they are going to leave her off it and see how she goes. She has been in air most of the day. I'm very proud of Amy; she knew she was ready to come off the driver and made sure the nurses knew as well.

Amy's feeds are being fortified again and so far she has been tolerating it. Amy has a mustard colour outfit on today and it really brings out the red tinge in her hair. I had a nice cuddle with Amy in the morning.

Wednesday 29 July 1998

Hailey 1,855 grams / Amy 1,453 grams

Amy is still doing well off the driver and hasn't required any oxygen as yet. She was having a few vomits so they have stopped fortifying her milk again. Her weight has been about the same for nearly a week. I hope she puts some on soon so I can give her a bath (at 1,500 grams). I gave Amy a wash and a cuddle in the morning.

Hailey now has two IVs in her forehead. She has been quite active now that she has all her limbs free. I gave Hailey a wash and a much-needed cuddle in the afternoon.

It broke my heart in the evening when I came in and saw Hailey had had some of her beautiful hair shaved in order to put a long line in through one of her veins in her scalp.

My darling Hailey, I'm sorry that you have to endure this. It doesn't appear to be bothering you, as you are still quite active. I will not take photos of you with the line in your scalp, because it is not fair to remind you of this. The doctors assure me it is not causing you any pain. I know your beautiful hair will grow back in time. I love you Hailey – Mummy xx

Thursday 30 July 1998

Hailey is quite active when she is awake. The IVs in her forehead have been removed because they tissued (this happens when the cannula moves from the vein and fluid builds up in the tissue), so she now has a golf ball sized lump there. The long line will last till Hailey no longer needs it, so her nutrition will go through it and she will still have one IV for her antibiotics. Her feeds will start again Monday or Tuesday. I just wish I could make things better for Hailey.

Amy is still doing well off the driver and no oxygen. Her feeds have been increased to 8 ml hourly which she appears to be tolerating. She has had a few desaturations today so I hope she is not getting tired of breathing. I had a nice cuddle with Amy in the afternoon.

Friday 31 July 1998

Hailey 1,860 grams / Amy 1,580 grams

Amy has been having several small desaturations, so has got some cot oxygen. I gave Amy a wash and a cuddle in the morning. We wrapped Amy up when we put her back in the cot and it seemed to settle her quite well.

Hailey is still getting upset that she is not being fed – hopefully for not much longer though. I gave Hailey a wash and a cuddle in the afternoon.

Trying to express my love for the girls is impossible. I'm so looking forward to having them home to be a family. I know we have many happy times ahead.

Month 4

August 1998

Saturday 1 August 1998

Hailey will hopefully start back on milk feeds tomorrow. It will be a slow process to get her back to full feeds then two hourly feeds. She has slept most of the day and looked quite peaceful. Hailey is certainly growing and developing. Hopefully, once she is over her infection, all we will need to concentrate on is her feeding. She will continue on her antibiotics till Wednesday or Thursday.

Amy's feeds have been increased to 9 ml hourly and are having fortifier added to them. She is still in a bit of oxygen (about 25%) but hasn't been desaturating like she was yesterday. Amy is getting much stronger, and is now able to lift and move her head from side to side and move and lift her body if she is on her tummy.

Both girls have very different colourings. Hailey has dark brown hair with an olive complexion and Amy has fair hair with a fair complexion. They are very individual in their looks and personalities.

Sunday 2 August 1998
Hailey 2,041grams / Amy 1,715 grams

Amy has been putting on weight too quickly, so she has been put back on diuretics to help reduce the fluid. She has still been requiring a small amount of oxygen, so hopefully the diuretics will help reduce fluid around her lungs and make breathing easier. She is tolerating her 9 mls of milk hourly which is good. I gave Amy a wash and a cuddle in the afternoon.

Hailey has finally been started back on feeds, which I'm sure will make her happy. She is on 2 ml four hourly, and this will be gradually increased. Hailey had also put on a bit too much weight, so she had one dose of a diuretic type IV drug. She did so much wee her cot linen needed to be changed also.

Today Amy is wearing a lovely dress I bought that was made for a Baby Born doll – it fits her quite well.

Monday 3 August 1998

Hailey has been tolerating her feeds well (2 ml four hourly). We have set up a feeding plan for her. We will try two breastfeeds a day, bottle feeds if she's awake and gavage feed (being fed through a tube in the nose or mouth directly into the stomach) if she's asleep. We tried the first breastfeed last night and she did okay. Each day she will get better. They will try turning Hailey's cot temperature down tonight to see if she holds her own temperature; if so, she will be moved to an open cot.

In the afternoon, Hailey's feeds increased to 4 ml four hourly, then at midnight it will be 8 ml four hourly.

Amy's feeds have been increased to 10 ml hourly. She has been sleeping most of the day. Her temperature has been on the lower side the last couple of days, so I hope she's not getting sick. Amy's salt supplement has been stopped to also help reduce her fluid.

I had a nice cuddle with both girls during the day. The girls have grown and changed so much that I've almost forgotten just how small they were when they were born.

Tuesday 4 August 1998 (13 weeks old)
Amy 1,678 grams

Amy's temperature has been a bit up and down. Her cot temperature has been turned down, so we will see what happens. Her oxygen requirements have gone down a bit, which is good. Amy had her eyes checked today and they are on the improve. She apparently got very close to surgery, but luckily she appears to have escaped it. She is still in the peak time of ROP, so I hope she continues to improve.

Hailey is continuously getting stronger. She had a bottle overnight and another at lunchtime which she took quite well. She looks good all dressed in some of her own clothes. They are holding off trying to move her to an open cot until she has finished her antibiotics (hopefully Thursday). Her feeds are being increased to 12 ml four hourly from midnight.

Brad had a very special afternoon. He did kangaroo care for the first time with Amy. She enjoyed it and fell asleep on Daddy's chest.

Wednesday 5 August 1998
Hailey 2,122grams / Amy 1,616 grams

Hailey has been tolerating her 12 ml four hourly feeds well, so at midnight it was increased to 16 ml four hourly. Her antibiotics will be continuing for another couple of days. I gave her another breastfeed today, but she played more than drank. I was able to give Hailey a bath in the afternoon which we both enjoyed. She still has the long line in her head which will stay there until she is on full milk feeds.

It's been an important day for Amy. After thirteen weeks in the neonatal intensive care unit, she has been transferred to the special care unit, which is great progress for her.

Lately I've noticed Amy's feet are turning outwards. The physio will see her next week and hopefully show me some exercise to help coax her feet back the right way. In the meantime I will try and keep her feet positioned using rolled up nappies.

I had a nice cuddle with Amy in the morning.

Thursday 6 August 1998
Amy 1,585 grams

Amy has had a bit of an unsettled day. They increased her feeds to 11 ml hourly but she didn't tolerate it and had a few vomits. Her feeds have been dropped back to 10 ml hourly. Her potassium was a bit low so she has been given a supplement. Low potassium can cause the gut to not absorb milk very well.

The doctors are getting a bit concerned at her consistent loss in weight (although it was mostly fluid) and are hoping they can find an even balance of medication, diuretics and milk for her to put on 'real' weight. I gave Amy a wash and a cuddle in the afternoon.

Hailey's feeds are now 24 ml four hourly which she is tolerating. Currently they are increasing her feeds by 4 ml every twelve hours. I'm not sure if they will go back to two or three hourly. She had two attempts at breastfeeding today and is getting a bit better each time.

In the evening, Hailey's feeds became 28 ml four hourly. Her antibiotics have been stopped and the IV removed. For the past four weeks, she has been on antibiotics for three, so hopefully this is the end of antibiotics for her.

Amy has still been doing a few vomits; I hope she is okay.

Friday 7 August 1998

Hailey 2,173grams / Amy 1,599 grams

Hailey has had her feeds reduced to three hourly which is better for her size. She is currently on 30 ml three hourly, and every third feed it is going up by 3 ml till it gets to full feeds of 39 ml three hourly. Once she is on full feeds, the line will be taken out of her head.

I will be trying her at the breast as often as possible so we can try to establish feeding as soon as possible. Hailey has taken a few bottles over the past few days.

Amy has still been doing a few vomits and her tummy has been a bit distended. They have stopped her fortifier again and hopefully this will fix the problem. She has put on a little bit of weight since yesterday.

Amy has been changed over to low-flow oxygen today; two small prongs in her nose with tubing taped to her face. It gives her a constant flow of oxygen, making it easier for her to breathe. It is better than cot oxygen because we can bathe her, cuddle her and open cot doors without worrying about depriving her of oxygen. Amy's oxygen at the moment is .025, which is good. Hopefully she will grow out of oxygen before she comes home, but if not, we will adapt to accommodate our precious Amy. Her feeding tube has been put into her mouth now.

Both girls look so happy and peaceful when they are asleep. I love being with them and watching them.

I gave Hailey a bath in the afternoon and Brad had a nice cuddle with Amy in the evening.

Saturday 8 August 1998

Amy 1,625 grams

Today was a very special day for both girls. Hailey has been moved to an open cot and Amy had her first bath. They have certainly come a long way in the past thirteen weeks. I feel that we are on our way to being home, hopefully in a couple of months.

Amy appears to have adapted well to the low-flow oxygen. She has a bit of nappy rash at the moment which is irritating her. Her tummy is quite distended, but she has been digesting her milk, hasn't been vomiting and is doing a lot of wees and poos. I hope her tummy settles down soon. I hope Amy enjoyed her bath and her bottom wasn't hurting too much. I had a nice cuddle with Amy in the afternoon.

Hailey appears to like her new bed. She needs to be able to hold her temperature to be able to stay in an open bed; if not she will have to go back to an Isolette. She is wrapped very snuggly and slept well during the day. She should be on full feeds by the end of the night. Hailey is on no drugs at the moment and she hasn't been desaturating. She is doing quite well with breastfeeding.

Sunday 9 August 1998

Hailey 2,075 grams

Hailey has been tolerating her feeds well of 40 ml every three hours. She has finally had the long line removed from her head. Hopefully for Hailey, all that is left is to establish her feeding, then she can come home. I gave Hailey a bath in the afternoon and a cuddle.

Amy is a bit of a mess at the moment. Her tummy is distended, her nappy rash has got worse with the blistering skin now peeling off and she has thrush in her mouth. My poor precious Amy. She had an abdominal X-ray done and it was clear. She also had a blood test done and there is no sign of infection. Hopefully her tummy will settle down soon. She is tolerating her feeds of 10 ml hourly okay. She has been in air quite a bit of the day, which is good. We have been nursing Amy without nappies to try and dry out her bottom. My precious Amy, I pray that you are better and stronger soon.

Monday 10 August 1998

Amy 1,672 grams

Amy is in much better spirits today. Her tummy has gone down and her bottom has improved. She has a nappy back on and is dressed. I'm sure this makes her more comfortable. I think Amy has an intolerance to the fortifier being put in my breast milk.

This is the third time she has had a swollen abdomen. Her tummy goes down in a couple of days each time they stop the fortifier, and then they start her on it again, but in about a week her tummy swells up again and we go through the process again. I have requested that no more fortifier be added to her milk.

Amy is still putting on weight which is good. I gave her a bath and a cuddle in the afternoon. She is still on the low-flow oxygen, but in air most of the time, which is excellent.

Hailey is continuing to do well. She is tolerating her feeds which are now 41 ml every three hours. She had a good breastfeed this morning. I found she was better when I had a nipple shield on because it gave her more to latch on to.

I keep debating about whether to continue trying to breastfeed, because I don't know if the girls are getting enough milk. I think we will try and establish them on breast and bottle.

Tuesday 11 August 1998 (14 weeks old)

Hailey 2,096 grams

Today was a very special day for Hailey and Amy. They have both been moved to Bay 3 – one more step closer to home.

Hailey has also ceased monitoring (the monitoring included her blood pressure, oxygen within the blood and breathing rate), so now she just has a gavage tube but nothing else connected to her. Hailey must establish feeding, then she can come home in possibly three to four weeks. She is continuing to do well with her two breastfeeds each day. Her feeds are now 44 ml three hourly.

Amy is being graded today to two hourly feeds of 22 ml which I hope she tolerates. She is almost weaning herself off the oxygen which is good. Amy is showing signs of having a real temper already. She is very determined. I had a brief but lovely kangaroo cuddle with Amy in the afternoon.

Wednesday 12 August 1998

Amy 1,697 grams

Amy is tolerating her two hourly feeds well. She has been in about 0.125 oxygen all day, which is okay. I gave Amy a bath and a cuddle in the afternoon. The last couple of days Amy has been very ratty in her Isolette. She needs to be 1,800 grams before she can go to an open cot, but we are going to try and move her sooner because I think she would be happier if she was wrapped up all the time on an open bed.

Hailey has been sleeping well most of the day. She had half her feed from a bottle this morning and last night. She has good sucking ability; she just needs to be able to stay awake long enough to have a feed. She is starting to stir every three hours.

Both girls appear happy in Bay 3. It is a lot more chaotic and you do more yourself, which is good, as there are more babies per nurse to be cared for. I think I will be spending more time at the hospital watching and doing things for my precious babies.

Thursday 13 August 1998 (100 days old)
Hailey 2,100 grams

Hailey has had her gavage tube removed. She is getting very clever and has been taking some full bottle feeds (46 ml). The plan for her is two breastfeeds a day, bottles if she is awake and one gavage feed overnight. I gave Hailey a bath in the afternoon.

Amy is slowly being weened into an open cot. She has been in constant oxygen of 0.125 since she came into Bay 3, which I'm not happy about. She can cope on her own, so I hope they give her a chance and she doesn't become too oxygen dependent. I had a nice cuddle with Amy in the afternoon.

Friday 14 August 1998
Full Term – 40-weeks gestation

Today is a day of celebration, as Hailey and Amy have reached their full term. It is wonderful that modern technology has been able to assist our babies to grow and develop outside the womb. We are very lucky to have such beautiful daughters.

Amy has had a special day herself. She has been moved to an open cot. Her weight is a bit less than what they usually like it to be when moved, so she must maintain her temperature or she will need to go back to an Isolette.

I have made a very difficult decision about Amy today. I have decided it would be better for her to be bottle fed instead of breastfed, as it requires less effort. I feel the easier I make it for her, the better, as she needs to preserve her energy for breathing and growing. I will still give her breastmilk and in time she may be strong enough to breast feed.

Hailey has been continuing with her feeding and improving each day. Next week I will probably start trying to give her three breastfeeds a day.

Saturday 15 August 1998

Hailey 2,112 grams

Hailey is continuing to do well with her feeding and is waking for most feeds. I gave Hailey a nice bath in the afternoon.

Amy has been able to maintain her temperature and is still in an open cot. She has had the low-flow taken off her to see how she goes without oxygen. I know she can do it. The bigger she grows, the stronger she is getting. Her feeds are now 24 ml two hourly. She took part of her feed from a bottle last night and tonight. I'm sure she'll get the hang of it. I'm very proud of Amy and her progress.

Both girls have come a long way. I finally feel like a mum now that I do most of the caring for the girls. I can't wait till they're home and we can be a family. Hailey and Amy are the most precious people in the world to me.

In the afternoon, Amy was struggling a bit too much without her oxygen, so I requested that she have the low-flow reconnected. She is in .0125 a litre of oxygen and has been a lot more settled. I just want what's best for Amy.

Sunday 16 August 1998

Amy 1,810 grams

Amy has hit four pounds. She has been much more stable since being back on the oxygen. It's only a small amount, but it helps her a lot. She has tried a few bottles and can suck well but her swallowing is a bit slow (she has her feeding tube in her mouth, so this doesn't help). I'm sure she'll coordinate suck/swallow soon. Amy is holding her temperature well in the open cot. I gave Amy a well enjoyed bath in the afternoon.

Hailey has had a couple of successful breastfeeds during the day. I'm going to try and breastfeed her each feed when I'm with her and bottles when I'm not, unless she is too tired, then she will be gavage fed. She's done well so far and hasn't had a gavage feed since 9 am yesterday.

Monday 17 August 1998
Hailey 2,124 grams

Things are moving quick at the moment, which is wonderful. Hailey has continued to do well with her feeding and has had all sucking feeds (breast or bottle) since Saturday morning. We are rooming-in with her on Tuesday and Wednesday night so I can give her all feeds, change her nappies and settle her back to sleep.

If she puts on weight, she may come home Thursday. This would be incredible, but I'm apprehensive about leaving Amy behind.

Amy has been graded to three hourly feeds of 38 ml, which she is tolerating well. We have started her feeding plan of three bottles per day. If she goes well, hopefully she may be home in four to six weeks. There is nothing I want more than having both my baby girls at home.

It will take Amy a little while to get the hang of bottles. She sucks well but just needs to coordinate swallowing. She has been in minimum oxygen all day.

Hailey had her immunisation in the afternoon so is being monitored for twenty-four hours in case she has a reaction.

I'm a very lucky mum – I cuddle both girls every day now and every alternate day I give them a bath.

Tuesday 18 August 1998 (15 weeks old)
Amy 1,844 grams

Amy has been taking her bottles quite well. It requires patience and can take about half an hour plus for her to finish her bottle. She sleeps peacefully and when she is awake she is alert. I gave Amy a bath in the afternoon.

Hailey had her eyes checked today. They are much improved and no longer show signs of Stage 1 ROP, so she shouldn't have future vision problems. She is doing well with demand feeding and wakes for a feed about every three hours. We are rooming-in with Hailey tonight, which should be fun.

Wednesday 19 August 1998
Hailey 2,146 grams

We had a good night of rooming-in with Hailey. She woke about 1 am, 5 am and then 8.30 am for a feed, which was good. Brad slept through it all though.

I weighed Hailey and gave her a bath in the morning. She has put on weight, which is excellent, so they are organising things to discharge her tomorrow. It will be nice to have Hailey home, and hopefully Amy may be home in about four to six weeks. Brad is starting his new job tonight, so I will be rooming-in with Hailey alone.

Amy is not being forgotten. I am trying very hard to establish her on bottles. I need to learn how to feed her successfully and she needs to be patient with me. Amy's eyes were checked today; one eye is greatly improved and the other is on the improve. She is still on twice daily eye drops and will be checked again in two weeks. She took a bottle from me in the evening, which made me exceptionally happy.

Thursday 20 August 1998
Amy 1,839 grams

Hailey discharged from hospital.
    Age: 15 weeks and 2 days old
    Length of stay: 107 days (6 days post-term)
    Weight: 2,150 grams
    Length: 45 cm
    Head circumference: 33 cm

Today was a very special day for Hailey – she came home. I shed tears of joy, and tears of sadness at leaving Amy behind.

Hailey arrived home about 5 pm and settled into home life quite well. I will end Hailey's chapter of hospital life here, now that she has reached the goal of home.

Amy had a bit of an unsettled day; I think she knew something different was happening. She had a couple of bottles during the day and did quite well. Amy's feeds are now 40 ml three hourly. I gave Amy a nice bath in the morning.

I'll miss not being able to spend as much time at the hospital with Amy, but I must try and establish and settle Hailey at home. Amy will be with me always though.

Friday 21 August 1998

Amy has had quite a settled day. Her oxygen has been very minimal, which is good. She slept through most of Hailey and my visit. I hope we can get her feeding established soon so she can come home and we can be a family. I love my girls so much; they are two very beautiful individuals.

I'll try and spend as much time with Amy as possible, but I need to be careful about keeping Hailey out in the cold night air.

Saturday 22 August 1998

Amy 1,868 grams

Amy made me very happy today. She drank all of her bottle in twenty minutes. I turned Amy's oxygen up before she started feeding and I believe this assisted her, because she didn't have to struggle with breathing and drinking at the same time. I gave Amy a relaxing bath in the afternoon.

I miss not being with Amy in the evenings but I need to be home with Hailey. I hate the thought of Amy not having visitors in the evening, but she must know how much I love her and think about her all the time.

Sunday 23 August 1998

We're trying to establish Amy's correct oxygen requirements. At the moment she is having .01 of a litre of oxygen, and when she is having a bottle her requirement is about .1 of a litre. She had another full bottle for me today, which made me very happy. She looks so beautiful and contented when she sleeps. I just love looking at her.

Monday 24 August 1998

Amy 1,893 grams

Amy has been continuing to do well with taking bottles. We are trying to give her alternate bottle and gavage feeds. If she is awake and demanding, a bottle will always be tried. She is starting to wake up for more feeds. Amy had a blood test done to check her calcium levels.

Tuesday 25 August 1998

The results from Amy's blood test yesterday show she is working hard to produce the calcium for her bones. They are doing an X-ray on her wrist to check her bone density. If necessary, she will be put on calcium supplements. They may review Hailey's bone density depending on Amy's X-ray results.

It is evident that Amy is growing, which is excellent. She is still doing well with taking her bottles.

Wednesday 26 August 1998

Amy 1,939 grams

Amy is continuing well with feeds. Since she has been having a bottle for every alternate feed, she has been able to drink all

40 ml in twenty to thirty minutes. Her wrist X-ray showed that her bones need more calcium. She would have got these extra nutrients from milk fortifier, but because she didn't tolerate it she is lacking calcium and phosphate. They will decide if she needs supplements and if they want to check Hailey.

I gave Amy a relaxing bath in the afternoon. She appears to enjoy her baths and I find it to be special bonding time for Amy and me.

Thursday 27 August 1998

Amy has been doing exceptionally well with sucking on bottles. She has had five bottles in a row. She is sleeping peacefully and often cries when her feed is due. I'm hoping she may be ready for home in two to three weeks. She is still requiring the same amount of oxygen and saturating high, which is good.

Friday 28 August 1998

Hailey 2,208 grams / Amy 1,968 grams

Amy is putting on weight at a steady rate. I have given her two bottles today. She had another blood test done to check her calcium level. I hope they establish soon if she needs supplements so she can get started.

I gave Amy a bath in the afternoon, which she wasn't too happy about because she was hungry. I love Amy so much. I hope she continues to do well and can come home soon.

Saturday 29 August 1998

Amy has been demanding bottles during the day, which is fantastic. She was saturating high so they turned her oxygen off, but her saturations dropped, so it was turned back on to .01. She had more blood tests to check her Vitamin D level. Apparently her phosphate level is high and her calcium low, so her body is working hard to maintain good bone formation for growth. It appears Amy will need some form of calcium and Vitamin D to help her grow.

Sunday 30 August 1998

Amy 2,040 grams

Amy has had a bit of a lethargic day. I hope she's not coming down with anything. She has had a few gavage feeds because she's been too tired to take a bottle. They are trying to wean her off the oxygen before she comes home (which will hopefully be soon), but I think she needs that tiny whiff to help her.

Amy's eyes were checked today and the report was good. I gave Amy a relaxing bath in the afternoon.

Monday 31 August 1998

I am getting very confused with Amy's bone density. Apparently her phosphate level is low, so they want to do more blood tests. We are still waiting for the results about her Vitamin D levels. I just want to get it all sorted out so she can be given the required supplements to help her grow.

Amy's blood test results show she is lacking phosphate, calcium and other minerals to help bone growth. These minerals are in the fortifier which Amy didn't tolerate. They have a few options to try, the first being half fortifier added to her milk. If she doesn't tolerate that, they will try her on alternate formula feeds or calcium and phosphate supplements added to my breast milk. They need to establish her on a suitable diet that she can have at home.

I had a lovely cuddle with both girls today, which appeared to help settle Amy.

Month 5

September 1998

Tuesday 1 September 1998 (17 weeks old)

Amy 2,041 grams

So far Amy has been tolerating the milk fortifier. Her feeds are now 43 ml three hourly. She is a bit anaemic at the moment, which is why she is lethargic. They want her to make her own blood and will only give her a top-up if her oxygen goes too high (because she is working harder trying to make new blood). Amy had her first trip outside of the Bay today when I took her to the bathroom for a bath.

Each day I'm getting more anxious about Amy coming home. I think it will be about two to four weeks away though. We need to establish her feeding, bone density and oxygen first.

Wednesday 2 September 1998

Amy has been more awake today. In the morning she was quite agitated, but settled when Hailey and I got to the hospital. We have been trying her with different teats and styles of bottles to help her feeding improve. It takes her about half an hour to have 43 ml, which is okay, but she gets very sleepy towards the end. The plan with Amy's feeding is all sucking feeds and maybe one gavage overnight if she is really sleepy.

Thursday 3 September 1998

Amy 2,062 grams

Amy's tummy has been a bit distended. She had an enema to clear her bowels and I hope this helps. I hope it's not another reaction to fortifier, because she needs it for her bones. The doctors are saying Amy has rickets, which is a disease caused by Vitamin D deficiency. It causes softening and distortion of the bones, often resulting in bowlegs. They are doing an ultrasound on her kidneys to check if there are calcium deposits on them. I think it's going to be awhile for Amy before she can come home, as they try and establish a solution to her bone formation. Her feeding I know I can handle at home, it just takes patience.

I gave Amy a bath in the afternoon. The ultrasound of Amy's kidneys showed a few white spots, but nothing to really worry about.

I'm getting very frustrated at the moment. I want Amy home so bad. Her feeding is very slow and she is having up to three gavage feeds a day. I wish there was something I could do to make it easier for her.

Friday 4 September 1998

Amy made great progress today. She is now on four hourly feeds of 60 ml, which she is tolerating well. She has been demanding more and taking her bottles quite well. The phosphate supplement has been ceased for now and so has her salt. Hopefully the fortifier is helping with her calcium levels and bone density.

Saturday 5 September 1998

Amy 2,087 grams

Amy is doing much better with bottles since her feeds were changed to four hourly. She hasn't had a gavage feed since 6 pm Thursday, which is good. I gave Amy a nice bath in the afternoon.

Sunday 6 September 1998 (Father's Day)

Amy is still coming along well. They have stopped her diuretics, so the only drugs she is on are Pentavite, Fergon and eye drops. The nurses are going to do a run soon to check her exact oxygen requirements and start planning for her to come home. She is very alert when awake. Amy is acting more like Hailey in her sleeping manner and wriggling up the bed.

Monday 7 September 1998

Amy 2,150 grams

The wheels have been put in motion to have Amy discharged. All going well, she will come home next Monday – I can't wait.

Her oxygen has been turned off today and they are doing a run to try and establish if and when she needs oxygen. Her saturation has been dropping to about 89, then she picks herself up, so we'll see. They did another blood test to check her calcium, so I hope that's under control. Brad, Hailey and I will room-in Friday night with Amy so I can feed her overnight.

Soon we will be a family at home and my dream will be fulfilled.

Tuesday 8 September 1998

Things change daily at the hospital. Now they are saying mid next week to discharge Amy. She didn't do as well as hoped off oxygen, so she will come home on oxygen at a rate of .125. This is higher than she really needs, but is the mandatory rate that babies get at home. In a couple of months, she should come off it cold turkey.

Her eyes were checked today and have improved even further, so her eye drops have been stopped. Amy's calcium and phosphate levels are much better, so now they have to establish a suitable diet for her at home so she gets enough calcium.

Wednesday 9 September 1998
Amy 2,210 grams

Amy's being moved today to Bay 1, which is good. She is putting on consistent weight and soon she will outweigh Hailey. She is having her immunisations today in the evening with the plan of discharge for Tuesday.

I learnt about her oxygen today and it shouldn't be too daunting at home. I gave Amy a bath in the afternoon to try and settle her because she was a bit grisly.

Thursday 10 September 1998

Amy had a bit of a lethargic day today, perhaps due to her immunisations last night. She was unable to finish a couple of her bottles, which is unlike her. She has bad nappy rash again and they are worried this is caused by the formula added to my milk. Amy has really been through a lot. I just want her home so I can cuddle her all day long and try to take away some of her pain.

Friday 11 September 1998
Amy 2,265 grams

Amy's bottom has blistered again, so the doctors have stopped the formula additive and she is having straight breast milk. Her feeds are now 62 ml four hourly. They are worried there is too much sugar in the formula, which is affecting her bottom. Amy is starting to demand her feeds, which is good.

I gave her a nice relaxing bath in the afternoon. The respiratory specialist saw Amy in the afternoon and is happy for her to go home on oxygen. He feels she will only need the oxygen for a couple of months and will see her on a regular basis. The oxygen probably won't be delivered till Tuesday, but we should be able to take her home Tuesday night – I can't wait. Brad, Hailey and I roomed-in with Amy tonight.

Saturday 12 September 1998

We had a good night of rooming-in with Amy. She demand fed every four hours which kept me on my toes. She had a very wakeful day and was a bit unsettled after being in the rooming-in room. She has started a new diet, which is breast milk with a bit of De-Lact (lactose free formula). This gives her the extra calcium and phosphate she needs but is not as rich as S26 formula. I hope she tolerates it okay.

Sunday 13 September 1998

Amy 2,330 grams

Amy has had a day of rest. I was very impressed with her when I gave her a bottle in the afternoon. It only took her fifteen minutes, then she had extra. She had a nice bath in the afternoon. Her bottom has improved after the nappy rash. She is tolerating her new feed so far, so I hope this continues.

Monday 14 September 1998

Well, it's happening. Amy's oxygen has been ordered for delivery at home tomorrow. All going well, we will be able to take her home tomorrow afternoon. She has had a good day and is continuing to take her bottles in a reasonable time.

She had blood tests done and they showed her calcium level is dropping again. Her diet has been changed back to breast milk and half fortifier, which they will supply for me at home.

Hailey and Amy had cradle photos taken today, so I hope they work out.

It's hard to believe that after nineteen weeks, it is almost over, and our two beautiful daughters will soon be home. We can finally shower them with the love, cuddles and kisses they deserve.

Tuesday 15 September 1998

Amy discharged from hospital.
   Age: 19 weeks
   Length of stay: 133 days (32 days post-term)
   Weight: 2,365 grams
   Length: 42 cm
   Head circumference: 33.5 cm
   Oxygen requirement: .125 of a litre

Hailey and Amy's hospital stay is now over, as they both have reached home. Brad and I are so lucky to have two beautiful daughters to love and cherish. We can now start our life as a family.

Milestones

Hailey

First crawled: mid-March 1999

First sat unsupported: 15 April 1999

First tooth appeared: 20 March 1999

Lost first tooth: 15 February 2005 (swallowed with breakfast)

First stood supported: early April 1999

First stood alone: 14 October 1999

First walked: 23 October 1999 (about eight steps alone) – 17 months old

First haircut: 17 September 1999

First word: Mum

First shoes: 6 December 1999 (white sandals size 5E)

Amy

First crawled: end of July 1999

First sat unsupported: 21 June 1999

First tooth appeared: 9 April 1999

Lost first tooth: 10 December 2003

First stood supported: November 1999

First stood alone: 3 March 2000

First walked: 22 March 2000 (too many steps to count) – 22 months old

First haircut: 6 October 2000

First word: Dada

First shoes: 20 April 2000 (brown leather boots Size 4E)

Vocal cord paralysis diagnosed: July 2001

Left-sided hemiplegia diagnosed (type of cerebral palsy): 24 October 2001 (first moon boot fitted)

Conclusion

Life never quite turns out as we think and hope it will. For as long as I could remember, all I ever wanted was to be a mum. I thought it was something that would come naturally once we made the decision to start a family. Why wouldn't it? We were educated on how not to fall pregnant, so falling pregnant sounded easy and so natural. Sadly, for us and many like us, this was not the case.

IVF became the best option for Brad and I if we wanted to have our much longed-for family. It was invasive, tiring, clinical and certainly not the way I hoped or wanted to conceive my children. We were very fortunate that after one failed attempt with three implanted embryos, our second attempt was successful. Again we had three viable embryos implanted, but only two 'took' and continued to develop into beautiful babies.

Apart from feeling very tired and experiencing a little morning sickness in the first trimester, my pregnancy went smoothly. I was working full-time and preparing for the arrival of not one but two babies at the same time. I opted to finish work at twenty-five weeks into my pregnancy, to give me plenty of time to prepare myself and our home. Sadly, I never got to finish work as planned.

Extreme prematurity was not something I had ever thought about or heard of. I knew babies could be born early, but not at twenty-five weeks. When my waters broke at twenty-four weeks and three days gestation, I had no idea what I was in for.

I was admitted to Waverley Private Hospital then transferred by ambulance to Monash Medical Centre, which was more equipped to handle such extremely premature babies. I was admitted to the private part of Monash, Jessie McPherson Hospital, where I was told I would remain until I had the babies, as I had to stay off my feet and be closely monitored. I was also at high risk of getting an infection, so it was believed hospital was the safest place for me.

I was happy to sit it out in that hospital room for as long as I had to if it meant my babies would be born healthy. But one week to the day, at just twenty-five weeks and three days gestation, I developed an infection and was very unwell. We were told by my obstetrician that the babies would have to be delivered that day, as I was too ill to continue the pregnancy.

That day was Tuesday 5 May 1998, one of the happiest and scariest days of my life. On the way to the delivery suite, I was quickly shown the neonatal intensive care unit and told this is where my babies will be brought after they are born – if they survive the birth.

My obstetrician attempted to induce a natural labour, but time and nature were against us. My health was deteriorating and the labour wasn't progressing as quickly as required. We were given two options: proceed with natural labour and risk losing the first baby as she was in distress but the second baby would be okay, or have an emergency caesarean which would give both babies the best chance possible, but risk my life (as I had an infection, opening me up could cause health complications). I felt there was no option, and straight away asked for a caesarean, as I could fight to get better, but my babies couldn't.

At 9.33 pm Hailey was born weighing just 670 grams, followed one minute later by Amy who weighed 592 grams. I didn't get to see the girls, as they were whisked away by the waiting medical teams so they could be assessed and ventilated to keep them alive. I went back to my room and it was at least twenty-four hours later that I got my first glimpse of the girls in their plastic bags.

Hospital life became the norm, but once we came home the journey continued with lots of medical appointments and follow-ups. We had weekly weigh-ins with the health nurse and ongoing medical appointments with the respiratory specialist, physiotherapist, paediatrician, speech therapist and occupational therapist. I didn't mind as I felt like the luckiest mum ever.

The girls and I joined a mothers' group, which was a great distraction from all the medical appointments. We opted to join the mothers' group with babies around the girls' corrected age, not their actual age. Their corrected age is the date they were due, which was 14 August, and their actual age is the date they were born, 5 May. We did this so they would not be so far behind in development, but be with babies at the same developmental stage as them.

As a group we continued on to playgroup. To this day I am still grateful that we did, as we have made lifelong friends who supported, guided, encouraged and stood by us.

Both girls had a lot of medical issues to deal with, but sadly for Amy, she suffered more. Amy was diagnosed with Chronic Lung Disease (CLD) whilst still in hospital. This disease is common in babies who are born before twenty-six weeks and weigh less than 1 kg, and it causes breathing and health problems. This saw her come home from hospital on oxygen, which she stayed on for approximately ten months. She was re-admitted to hospital three times in eighteen months with respiratory conditions such as RSV (respiratory syncytial virus). Each time she took it in her stride.

One episode saw Amy and I head off to hospital in an ambulance during the evening. We managed to be so quiet that Hailey slept through us leaving and didn't know till the morning that Amy and I were in hospital. Amy went on to suffer from asthma, but as she got older the asthma symptoms slowed down, and by the time she hit her teens, the asthma had gone away altogether.

Feeding was really difficult for Amy as a baby, as she burnt her calories breathing and fighting infections (another issue of CLD). She was often too tired to drink from her bottle. This would see me in tears of frustration, trying to keep her awake and drinking. Hailey was successfully breastfed until she was about nine months old, then I swapped her to bottles. At times it was quite challenging balancing the girls' feeding routines.

Amy always tired much quicker than other children her age, and even had a special bean bag in the corner of the classroom in the early years of primary school, so she could have a rest when needed. She still needs more rest than Hailey to get her through the day.

Amy learnt to manage her left-sided hemiplegia (caused by an injury to the part of the brain controlling muscle movements of the limbs) with lots of support from us. We did lots of movement and play with her at home so she learnt to use her left arm and leg correctly. We also spent a lot of time with the physiotherapist and did hydrotherapy to assist her to walk. Amy had to wear a moon boot on her left leg every night in bed for many years to stop the muscles from stiffening up during the night. After all this treatment, there is no sign of a limp when Amy walks, something the specialist told us to expect.

Amy played competition basketball for nine years and watching her play made me so proud. Here was a child who was given short odds to survive, told she would walk with a limp and was unable to use her left arm, and here she was running the length of a basketball court, dribbling the ball between both hands.

Both girls had ongoing eye issues, requiring glasses to be worn at different stages of their development.

Hearing was also another issue for Amy. It seemed the older she got, the more it deteriorated. By the age of eight, she was relying on two hearing aids to help her. In an attempt to get answers and help for Amy's deteriorating hearing, I went to four different specialists to find someone who could help. We eventually did find a surgeon, who did surgery on Amy at The Royal Children's Hospital in May 2007. He removed the 'hammer' bone in her left ear that had fused together and was stopping the vibration so sound couldn't get through. He replaced the bone with a small metal shunt.

Amy went from relying on two hearing aids to none. This will restrict Amy from doing any high-altitude or deep-sea activities, but she could finally hear without hearing aids. She just needs to be cautious of any sudden head movements, so as to not dislodge the shunt.

Hailey had her fair share of obstacles in the early years, but overcame each and every one of them without a great deal of incidence. Her gut condition that caused her problems in hospital has continued to cause her issues over the years, but she has learnt to manage it well.

Amy has had to endure left-side vocal fold (cord) paralysis. This has affected her voice quality, articulation and volume. Because the cords don't fully close and vibrate when she talks, her voice can sound breathy and at times hoarse. She is unable to yell and raise her voice (at times this is a good thing).

During their younger years, Hailey would often act as interpreter for Amy and speak for both of them when they were at playgroup or kindergarten. This helped create an even stronger bond between the girls. I still notice that the girls at times tend to use 'us' or 'we' more often than 'I' when they want something.

In primary school, Amy had an aide with her in the playground, because if she got stuck on the play equipment she was unable to call for help. She was fitted with a microphone through The Royal Children's Hospital, which she used in the classroom in her early years of primary school to help project her voice. She was also prone to choking on her drinks and small pieces of food, so we made sure she was supervised during snack and lunchtime at school and also at home. Amy never let her voice hold her back, and joined the primary school choir. She was even choir captain when she was in Grade 6.

Often when someone meets Amy for the first time, they ask if she has a sore throat or a cold, due to the sound of her voice. If it's a person she will never see again, often she will just say yes, she has a sore throat. If it's someone she will be seeing again, she'll explain that she has a paralysed left vocal cord and this is how she sounds. I am so proud of how Amy has dealt with this – she has amazing self-esteem.

It was always my aim to socialise the girls as much as possible to aid their development and social skills, and to give them all the possibilities I could to enjoy their lives. As well as our mothers' group, we joined the multiple birth group, attending morning teas with other multiple families. The girls attended a playgroup especially for multiple children and siblings when they were three and four years old. We also attended a playgroup with other parents who'd had long-term babies in Monash Medical Centre, and again lifelong friendships were created.

Both Hailey and Amy were always encouraged to participate in sports and out of school activities. Hailey did dancing for eleven years. She did tap, jazz, hip hop and ballet, and enjoyed every moment of it. I was so proud at every end of year concert. I had tears in my eyes as I watched her perform on stage and thought, this is my little girl who fought so hard to be here.

Hailey also sang in the primary school choir, and she played the violin throughout primary and the early years of high school. In primary school, she played in the school band, and again I was so proud of her every time I watched her perform. Amy did tennis lessons from approximately age six to nine, then had to choose between tennis and basketball due to a clash of training times, and chose basketball.

High school saw a new era for Hailey and Amy. By this stage their medical conditions were well under control and they were ready for a new challenge. The first high school they went to didn't offer what they wanted academically, but during their time at the school they both participated in the Rock Eisteddfod, which was a fabulous experience.

They changed schools at the end of Year 8 to a school better suited to them. Amy then changed schools again, halfway through Year 11 to a TAFE school to do VCAL, an alternative to VCE. This was the first time Hailey and Amy had been separated at school. They missed each other greatly, but I saw them both grow and develop in their own right. It was definitely a good move in many ways for both girls.

Holidays were and still are a highlight of each year, as fun is always had and great memories created. Time spent with cousins and family friends has seen many fun times and are still enjoyed today.

For years we corrected the girls' age so they didn't appear too far behind in development of other children the same age as them. I don't really remember when we stopped doing this, but now apart from being quite slight for their age and Amy's voice, there is no indication of their early start to life.

Birthdays have always been well-celebrated in our house. Each year on 5 May I make the day as special as I can for Hailey and Amy. At the same time, I feel a sense of sadness as I reflect on that day in 1998 and the days and months that followed.

During the girls' younger years, we always had a themed party with friends and family, which saw much laughter and fun. To give the girls their own special day (away from being a twin) we celebrated their 'anniversary', the day they each came home from hospital. The girls would get a gift on their anniversary day and have a small celebration of their choice. The girls have now outgrown celebrating anniversaries, but growing up it was exciting, as it was a day just for them. They are still reminded each year of the day that they came home from hospital, as to me that was the date I truly felt the babies were mine.

Where are they now?

Watching Hailey and Amy develop outside the womb was both fascinating and frightening. Not many parents get to see this. At times I wouldn't change a thing about the girls' early start to life, and at other times I get sad and angry at what they went through. We couldn't change the past so we made the most of it. During the 133 days the girls were in hospital, they showed me what determination and courage truly meant. I somehow found my inner strength at the same time.

The girls and I have developed an incredibly tight bond. I was so grateful that they fought so hard to stay with me that I wanted to give them every opportunity I could. The early years were full of doctors' appointments and therapy sessions, but the most important part of our days were the playing, laughing, singing and socialising we did. It was all this that helped shape Hailey and Amy into who they are today.

Along the way I noted down what they wanted to be when they were older and what they were interested in at the time.

When I grow up I want to be a ...

28 October 2003 (5 years, 5 months old)

Hailey
- ♥ Doctor
- ♥ Ice skater
- ♥ Princess
- ♥ Surfer
- ♥ Roller skater

Amy
- ♥ Ice skater
- ♥ Nurse
- ♥ Queen
- ♥ Police officer
- ♥ Roller skater (so I can go down the road on them)

6 March 2008 (9 years, 10 months old)

Hailey
- ♥ Doctor

Favourite colour: Purple
Favourite activity: Dancing

Amy
- ♥ PE Teacher

Favourite colour: Pink
Favourite activity: Playing basketball

Where are they now?

As with most children, their interests and friendships changed quite regularly along the journey from toddler to pre-teen to teenager and now to adulthood. However, there are some interests that have stayed the same and there are some very special friends who have always been there and continue to be here for Hailey and Amy.

I am so proud of the young ladies that Hailey and Amy are. They are different but the same. There has not been one stage in the girls' lives which I have not enjoyed sharing with them. As they are embarking on their journey into adulthood, I am excited about where the future will take them. Both girls are a combination of each other – smart, sassy, kind, funny, caring, loving, and very passionate about the other. They do have disagreements, but they don't last long.

Hailey and Amy have just turned twenty and are enjoying their lives.

Hailey is in her second year of university, undertaking a Bachelor of Health Science/Arts. She has a part-time job with Bakers Delight and has been there for over three years. She enjoys reading and spending time with her friends doing a variety of things. She especially has a love of flowers and nature. Hailey bought her first car, a Suzuki Swift, in August 2016 and got her licence seven months later. This has given her so much independence and an opportunity to do more things.

Amy completed a Diploma in Events Management at the end of 2017, and is now ready to embark on a career in events. She has always loved bands and live music, going to as many concerts as she can; it doesn't matter if they're a small local band or a large international band. Amy has had a few part-time jobs, including waitressing, and spent two years working at the local fish and chip shop. She is still learning to drive and will hopefully have her licence sooner rather than later. She enjoys spending time with friends, her boyfriend and pursuing her love of music.

Both girls have brought so much joy to my life. I am incredibly proud of who they are and the resilience they have. Together the three of us have created amazing memories, made incredible friends, loved and cherished our extended family, felt sadness when our first dog Clyde passed away, and happiness when our second dog Koda came into our lives. We have lost family members along our journey, and some very special friends too, each time reminding us of just how precious life is.

What a journey it has been so far. The world is at your feet Hailey and Amy, and I can't wait to see where it takes you.

www.ingramcontent.com/pod-product-compliance
Lightning Source LLC
Chambersburg PA
CBHW031123080526
44587CB00011B/1089